Spectral Realms

No. 3 ‡ Summer 2015

Edited by S. T. Joshi

The spectral realms that thou canst see
With eyes veil'd from the world and me.

"To a Dreamer," *H. P. Lovecraft*

SPECTRAL REALMS is published twice a year by Hippocampus Press,
P.O. Box 641, New York, NY 10156 (www.hippocampuspress.com).
Copyright © 2015 by Hippocampus Press.
All works are copyright © 2015 by their respective authors.
The cover, "Tunnel Fiend 6," is copyright © 2015 by Rabban.
Cover design by Barbara Briggs Silbert. Hippocampus Press logo
by Anastasia Damianakos.

ISBN 978-1-61498-147-3   ISSN 2333-4215

Contents

Poetry

Song of the Rushes

M. F. Webb

Recall I must the northern wind
That sings upon the grass
And fans in waves the cattails where
My old companions pass
And color deep and simple shines
Through old cathedral glass.

How is it that these things with souls
Can breathe so cruel confined—
No music but machinery,
No passage not defined—
And look at nothing but the ground
And never know the sky?

I cannot understand their ways,
Their constant sorrowing,
Apart from evening blue and wild
When every bird takes wing—
Such lure and lamentation, they
Compel my soul to sing!

In Fits of Wildest Dreaming

K. A. Opperman

In fits of wildest dreaming,
When demons all were teeming,
And scheming
To conquer midnight's throne,
I tossed in deepest slumber,
Through nightmares without number,
To cumber
The more, with awful groan,

My bed of silken scarlet.
A harpy-wingèd harlot—
A starlet
From courts of white Selene—
Seemed hellishly to hover
About me like a lover,
And cover,
With kisses so obscene,

My body, helpless sleeping!—
It seemed that she was reaping,
And keeping,
My soul with every kiss!
The succubus embraced me,
In ghostly beauty faced me,
To taste me,
And let me dream of bliss.

But there was scarce of pleasure,
No amorous red measure
To treasure,
Within my poisoned pulse;
For restless woes and worries
Swirled round me like lemures,
Or flurries
Of leaves that soon convulse

In graying autumn grasses,
As pensively there passes
Of lasses
The saddest of them all—
Poor Vespertina's specter,
When purple dusk has decked her,
Her nectar
Gone all to bitter gall.

And all the ghouls were howling,
The moonlit tombs befouling—
An owling
Made much of mournful moan—
When I was wildly dreaming,
And demons all were teeming,
And scheming
To conquer midnight's throne.

Inheritance

Christina Sng

She drove up the long driveway.
Whispers from the dead sang to her,
Ushering her up to the house.
Her inheritance. Presumed haunted,
But she did not believe in
Such superstition.

Turn back, turn back,
Or die like the rest.

The voices sang in her head,
Turning the corner around
The massive mansion, now
Moldy and grimy with age
And disrepair. She parked
The car and walked up
The massive steps meant for
A giant.

Go away, go away,
We do not want to play.

She stabbed the key into the lock.
It protested with a creak
But she shoved it open
Anyway. The lights were
Not working, despite

10

The electricity having been
Turned on that morning.

Tick, tock, we will
Pluck your heart out.

Her heart pounding,
She switched on the lamp
And took tentative steps.
The first floor was empty
But she heard a door slam,
Echoing like a concussion.

Come, come,
Come to the basement.

Yes, that was where
All the bad things happened.
The door was ajar. A faint
Light shone from beneath.
Each step creaked as she
Walked down. And there it was,
Shiny and clean.

Machines to scare people,
Keep them away. So I can play.

She remembered this place.
And she remembered him.
The sweets and the toys,
All to lure her here. For terror.
And his sick pleasure.
There he sat, back
Facing her, watching an
Old video with intent
Scrawled all over his face.

Old baseball bat. You won me
Trophies. Now do me a solid.

She swung and it connected
With his skull. Over and over
Till there was no more of it.
She walked from the house,
Smiling. Behind her, plumes
Of vermillion and red lit up
The night sky. In a month,
She received the insurance cheque.

Rebuild, rebuild,
And start over again.

Rune

Wade German

Now evening enters without sound
And banishes the noise of day.
In sudden silence, vast, profound,
An incommunicable name
Is uttered at night's portal way
Through which the shadow world evolves,
And spectral entities reclaim
The kingdom that the day dissolves.

Emerald moons and stars emerge
Above silentious land below
Where darkness reigns as demiurge,
Whose worship demon, ghoul, and witch
Attend as acolytes who know
The very silence is a rune—
A psalm of seances, by which
The shadows of the world commune.

Preserves

G. O. Clark

In her basement,
across from the old coal
burning furnace,

thirteen shelves
of home canned goods
from the garden.

Summer vegetables,
preserved for winter tables.
Jams and jellies aplenty.

Perfectly pickled
rodents, frogs, birds, and
long-lost pets.

She's expert at canning
the shallow-rooted: the warm
and cold-blooded.

Her best-of-show
rest upon some special shelves
back in the shadows:

human fetuses
abandoned by her coven
sisters, sealed and

saved for the Master,
his aborted progeny preserved
in the cellar cold.

Barley Night

Jonathan Thomas

Break o' day, the sun god sat
On the maidstone like a hat.
A sign, a sign since we were born
That time has come to plant the corn.

Thistle sprouting in the field,
Wintertime at last must yield.
But one thing must still be done
To win the favor of the sun.

Have no fear, you'll be all right
If you live through barley night.
Have no fear, you'll be all right
If you live through barley night.

Priest is casting holy bones
Out in front of every home.
As they fall he reads the will
Of the gods for good or ill.

Heaven only talks to him.
Barley day is always grim.
Would that fate had granted we
Should have a captive enemy.

Have no fear, you'll be all right
If you live through barley night.
Have no fear, you'll be all right
If you live through barley night.

End of day, the sun goes down
On the hagstone like a crown.
Priest appears with grease and dung
To anoint the chosen one.

Grab a stone or grab a stick.
If it must be done, be quick.
God decrees it from on high,
Bread for all, if one will die.

Have no fear, you'll be all right
If you live through barley night.
Have no fear, you'll be all right
If you live through barley night.

To the field we all repair,
Scatter blood and body there.
Quaff enough of holy brew,
You may forget the things you do.

Rising sun will smile to greet
Rising smell of raven meat.
By the grace of barley night,
Sun will bless us with his light.

Have no fear, you'll be all right
If you live through barley night.
Have no fear, you'll be all right
If you live through barley night.

Ode to Hecate

Liam Garriock

In some hell-ruined land I wander,
In search of the Queen of Ghosts.
The ember skies above brood with thunder
As I traverse the charred wastelands
In insatiate pursuit of the phantom hosts
From elder realms smothered by scorching sands.
Lo! amidst the sweltering desolation
I finally see the goddess of damnation.

O Hecate, send me to the cool moon
Whence I may suckle from thy breasts
The desired powers of necromancy and sorcery
Untamed. The sun shall sink soon,
So let us go to the lunar city
Where thy father, Life-in-Death, eternal rests.

A Shuddery Tale

Charles Lovecraft

"I shall always see those steps in my dreams . . ."–H. P. Lovecraft

I held the torch above my head at twelve,
And then descended into earth at will.
The musty stairs just seemed to dig and delve
Much deeper into nameless pits until
I found a cavern filled with eye-like coals.
Polyps of strange stone bent to look and hear.
The faceless rubbery things with lurid holes
For eyes now filled me with disturbing fear.

How horrible they were in their intent
To *sniff* I shudder, even now recall,
Whilst polymorphous avenues of trees,
Or what had seemed mere trees, wrung branches tall
And quivering to the air, with arms that bent
And moved and wriggled in my blood with ease.

Arcane Stars

DJ Tyrer

The arcane perturbations of the planets
Those wandering stars that dance through the sky
Mirrored by tiny, invisible movements of distant suns
And the more curious motions of dark stars unseen
Render a certain dread alignment
That coming together in blaspheming congress
Called by hidden savants the day
When the stars are right

Northern Lights

Mary Krawczak Wilson

The surreal green of the northern lights
Cast upon me an eerie uncertainty
As to my impending mortality;
The glow immersed me in a terrified fright.

Where was the core of my heart
I heard no sound nor beat;
I felt not the cold nor the heat;
Where were my words?—they all fell apart.

The mono-colored canvas
Enclosed itself on me,
Wrapping its tentacles incessantly
Until I submerged into an abyss.

No light, no sound, no health, no wealth.
Why did these elements conspire
To grant me a fate so dire
As an illusory and amorphous death?

Always Look under the Bed

Mark McLaughlin

If you're well-versed in Arkham history,
you know of Walter Gilman and his doom.
The Witch House was his chosen mystery—
a labyrinth hid in an attic room.
A student, he sought secrets most arcane
and met Keziah Mason and her beast.
Their evil nearby drove the lad insane.
Before long he became Brown Jenkin's feast.
If only he had looked under the bed!
That action would have changed his sorry fate.
Another door led far from witchy dread:
the laundry chute, a hidden mystic gate.
Although that dusty passage wasn't large,
he could have fled to Cleopatra's barge.

The Cave of Ebon Boughs

D. L. Myers

A choking fog obscured my panicked sight,
    And all about me blighted shadows danced,
    As if infernal harpies soared and pranced
Beyond a churning scrim of mist-fouled night.
And then a parting of the mist revealed
    That all around me twisted branches twined
    Into a net through which the moonlight shined,
A ghostly glow that in the air congealed.

Then through that cave of ebon boughs, I fled—
    Those horrid shadows pouncing at my heels—
    The branches high above me like black eels
That drank the brume and on the moonlight fed;
    Until in utter blackness, cold and blind,
    I froze in terror body, soul, and mind.

The Empty Room

Darrell Schweitzer

I dreamed that I lay in my bed,
while loved ones and friends
and then strangers looked down
on me with expressions of concern, grief,
and finally ill-concealed boredom,
while they carried away everything that was mine:
clothing, books, files, pictures from the walls,
even the plastic model airplane I'd built when I was twelve
and managed to preserve all these years;
and when it was all gone I saw myself diminish
beneath the sheet until nothing remained.

Then I awoke from that dream
and stood in the brightly sunlit room,
glanced around at the empty closet, featureless walls,
and the bare mattress, and I said to the landlord,
"Okay, I'll take it."

Dolls

Jason V Brock

Prancing glumly
up battered stairs,
Eyeless dolls
throw shadows
cold and long
onto decaying walls—

I watch them with fear:
Silently in awe
as I see the fading flicker of
my lamp
softly glow on their terrible
dress buttons.

Numb with dread,
I cringe in my fruiting madness . . .

Prancing glumly
up battered stairs,
Eyeless dolls
throw shadows
cold and long
onto decaying walls—
So begins the horrifying
Hop Macabre—

BEHOLD!
The elastic insanity of
Porous memory fragments
Falling into the
Dream pool
Of forgotten love . . .

Numb with dread,
I cringe in my fruiting madness . . .
The bats of lunacy
flitting in my head . . .

Prancing glumly
up battered stairs,
Eyeless dolls
throw shadows
cold and long
onto decaying walls–
So begins the horrifying
Hop Macabre–
The end of the Universe
Is in the mitten hands
Of soulless effigies made of
rags . . .

I observe their devil dance
And love of nothing in the tiny,
perverse room:
First one,
Then another,
Still a third—
The hopscotch of horror ensues
To Humanity's trumpet
of doom . . .

Numb with dread,
I cringe in my fruiting madness . . .
The bats of lunacy
flitting in my head . . .
How I got here is a
Mystery:
I pray to the loving God above that
I live through this reverie . . .

Prancing glumly
up battered stairs,
Eyeless dolls
throw shadows
cold and long
onto decaying walls—
So begins the horrifying

Hop Macabre–
The end of the Universe
Is in the mitten hands
Of soulless effigies made of
rags . . .
As they plummet–
One by one–
Into the void of Fate, then:
I am entranced by their hideous
Music of terror:
SCREAMING DOLLS AT THE WORLD'S END!

Suddenly,
I am overtaken by the satanic
Clown:
Appearing from my childhood
subconscious,
His menace is manifest by
Rending my flesh with shark-like teeth . . .
Blackness!

For Neil Gaiman and Thomas Ligotti

Painted Ladies

David Barker

The old man lives alone
in the derelict Victorian mansion,
his wife having left him
so many years ago it's like
she never was there. He misses
his daughter more, and
although she's a grown woman now
with a life of her own, he keeps
her dolls on display,
lined up on a high shelf
in her former bedroom.

Loneliness marks his days and
casts long shadows over his evenings.
His only solace comes
when, in the wee hours,
gramophone music once more
echoes though the upstairs chambers
and the decorous shades
of girls who worked and died there
when it was the town whorehouse
a century ago or more
traipse merrily down the halls,

flickering candles in their hands,
on errands of pleasure and comfort
to gentlemen callers—

And on those precious nights when
one ghostly tart or another
shambles into his room to
share his wintry bed.

Brownfields

(for Mark S.)

John Mundy

They call them Brownfields. Old crumbling factories, rotting gas stations, long-emptied dry cleaning establishments, diseased shells of commerce; businesses once thriving with meaningful activity but now mere desolate spectres of urban decay, lost in a hopelessly protracted limbo of legalities and litigation, sitting undisturbed atop polluted and poisoned land. They cannot be sold or transferred or converted; even attempted ecological cleanup is not a viable option for many of these sardonic Temples of Desolation. The rare *official* activity that disturbs their slumber (and their slumber must be a distressing one) is a lone local patrol car that shines its searchlight over the poisoned grounds in the quietude of night, enforcing a desultory and sporadic inspection, far from rigorous. Other activities, however, occur as well: the occasional arrival of the furtive or defiant: the squatters, the addicted, the homeless, all species of drifters, deviants and vagabonds, all who would take shelter from the cold and wet whenever and wherever Chance should offer it. Looters, too, may visit in search of some pitiful prize even though all wire, copper, brass and other scavengable material has invariably been stripped from such shells.

But what of other less familiar, less *easily* defined opportunists? What shadows willingly employ such grounds through the heart of a freezing winter or the long parched days of a withering summer? What purposes are served here and for what ends? A clownish and terrified figure, a luckless hobo perhaps, dressed in pathetic tatters, runs stumbling and shrieking from a factory now itself a corroded husk of poisons like the batteries it once made in a distant past. This transient sought shelter from a darkly pouring sky with the aid of one of his more prized possessions, a torsion wench, but found no welcoming dry refuge inside the black featureless walls . . . only a reeking abattoir instead.

So I ask you again, Doctor: What sacrifices are made in these unholy places, these shrines to Abandonment and Decay? And by what abominable hands?

Even Madness Cannot Hide

Ashley Dioses

The murmurs blow across the barren land
Of dim Carcosa, spoke from spectral lips.
A stillness wraps me with its wintry hands;
A strange awareness heightens, then it slips.

A weakness creeps and slithers deep inside,
From the foreboding presence of the King.
A torment even madness cannot hide
Arises, and I crave what Death would bring.

I kneel on bended knee and bow my head,
Yet such a power upward pulls my face.
I see behind the Pallid Mask, and red
And yellow fire engulfs me, from His Grace . . . !

The land is flooded by my wails and cries,
His voice triumphant in the flaming light.
His searing fire inflates to monstrous size
As I fall down the black abyss of night.

Revelation

Fred Phillips

Our ship made landfall on a distant globe
To finish work that had yet to be done;
Our mission was the depths of space to probe
And bring back proof that we were not alone.
Among us pundits skilled in ancient lore
Who could glyphs long-lost read and comprehend,
To cast their light on what had been before
And add to learning, to which there's no end.
Altars in their crumbled courtyards lent
An air of mystery wherever found,
And we learned for what purpose they were meant
And felt a chill upon that alien ground.
But one small mote of space had we revealed;
The rest lies still in mystery concealed.

Daemon Insectarium

Chad Hensley

Wasp woman from the thorax up with breasts,
Tight metasoma striped yellow and black.
Two six-jointed legs inviting all guests.
Pulsating stinger ready to attack.

Swarms of ant men have mandibles that twitch,
Human hands grip wicked homemade weapons.
Bloated red queen guarding giant mound niche.
An insect monstrosity that beckons.

Woman wasp flutters folded, fanlike wings.
Giant monarch butterflies high above
Extend a tendriled proboscis that clings
Wrapping around the ant men like a glove.

Mountainous spider howls with mouths in dismay,
Larger misshapen shapes move toward the fray.

Sorcerers in Love

Don Webb

Their love was
a collision of dreams
    intersecting somewhere above their black hearts.
As these dreams passed through
    one another
    they made great holes.
What had begun as pinpricks
    became great gaping holes.
And when the dreams had thoroughly
    passed through each other
    and found new targets,
    great black blood stained the yellow day.
And each died bleeding
    in the baffled arms of
    their newly intended victims.

Moonrise

Christina Sng

Moonrise over the horizon.

I glance at my pack, ready to turn.
They stretch and grunt as the dance
Of pain and broken bones begins.

Soon we loom over the mountain peak
Channeling the moon. Our furred pelts
Glisten like sunlight on dew.

The howl echoes across the valley.
A battle cry from our alpha,
Our god, summoning us for war.

Tonight we rise against the humans.
Tonight we take back our world.

The Game of Cat and Dragon

Pat Calhoun

After a story by Cordwainer Smith

The dragons loved the dark and would die in bright light.
So the people made pinlight grenades of pure white
Hell, to launch at attackers in the depths of space.
But starship crews went insane—chaos in each face,

For something about the dragons fried earthly brains
When they had time to come closing in. So humans
And cats were paired as a team: felines had the speed
To blast the bombs before sanity died. Indeed,

The tide began to turn in this interstellar
War, though battles were still fierce. One dragon got near
Underhill's mind, and its merest touch tore a wound,
Crazy blistering pain as his consciousness burned,

Till five photonuclear grenades burst, filled space
With dragon-melting blaze, flung by his fabulous
Lady May. He felt her feral elation at
The kill, and her thanks. Maybe she was just a cat,

But to him she was faster than thought, courageous,
Gloriously graceful, beautiful, and wordless,
And never asking more than to be his partner.
Where would he ever find a woman to compare?

Lovers' Wine

Stanley Gemmell

Contained in this purple red liquid
An evening's worth of bitter tears
Verses dispossessed of hope
Love with nothing left to fear,
I drink because you have left me
And gone far to live among the dead
Where my trembling hand cannot reach you
Among the dust remains my friend.

I planted a vineyard upon your grave
It yields a large quantity of wine
Each year grape-sugar mixes with despair
And he who drinks it goes insane.
Such was our love that all who drank
The poison worked its charm
Normal wine it seemed
But 'twas infused with love's gall.
And so each year I sheathed my sorrow
In yet another foul deed
At the scene of each crime
The black flame of our seed
Birthed a new death.

And so decades have passed
And no one knows the counter-spells
To this necromancy of hate,
Which can flourish in any clime

Any season—future, present or past.
But now my own fate is sealed
I have drunk the death
Of my love for you,
My child and bride of youth
I—an old man in decay.

What is this I see?
You come to me in pearled, black wings
Singing an aria bearing my name,
And all those I've killed flank to thee
With vengeful menace in burning eyes . . .
Oh burning Christ,
Whose white eyes are singing
Of justice dire, grim, complete!
Oh judgement fierce,
Angels of wrath, my eyes
Can no longer see,
I drink this goblet
Which has become a
Murderous simile:
Your name flows from me
In choking blood and bile . . .
Bitter wine which from the grave
Shall age a long, long while.

Childe Jackson Drake

Adam Bolivar

Childe Jackson to the dark house came,
The house in Shepherd's Wood.
His mother's dam once bore that name;
The taint ran in his blood.

He journey'd far to Shepherd's House,
Around his neck a Key,
An heirloom from his grandmother,
A haunted legacy.

Ten ravens perched upon the roof,
A gable for their nest,
And at the door an owl beseech'd,
"Who are you? What's your quest?"

"Why, I am Drake, the son of Jack,
Just journeyed from the dell.
I seek Yᵉ Olde, Yᵉ Shepherd Black,
To save my soul from Hell."

The Owl watched him with glowing eyes
That in the darkness see.
"If you are of the blood of Jack,
Then you will have a Key."

So Drake produced the Silver Key,
Which fit into the door,
And strode into the Shepherd's House,
Boots tapping on the floor.

The ebon hall in Shepherd's House
Was dark and wide and cold.
Its denizen lived all alone,
And some called him Yᵉ Olde.

"I am Yᵉ Olde, Yᵉ Shepherd Black,
An Angell was my dam;
I welcome Drake, the son of Jack,
For I your cousin am.

"The Sisters Wyrd are much a-feared,
For Madness bubbles up.
Black horsemen ride with beasts astride
Unless you win Yᵉ Cup.

"Yᵉ White Cup lies beyond Nine Gates,
To which there are Nine Keys.
I'll give you these Nine Keys to Hell,
The Sistren to appease.

But in return, I ask a price,
The Emerald in Y^e Cup.
Bring it to me, my cousin dear,
Or Hell will eat you up."

Then screech'd Y^e Owl: "The deal is done!"
And Drake turned the First Key
To open up the Gate of Time,
A door where none should be.

He crossed the Gate into a reed,
Where stood the House of Hare.
A roof of straw and walls of sod:
Y^e Rampant Hare lived there.

"Well met," declared Y^e Rampant Hare.
"I'll pour us both some tea.
I'll help you find the Second Gate;
To find the HWOL chase me.

"To blackest Hell I'll lead you sure.
From you I have one need,
A patch behind your noble house
To overgrow with weed."

So Jackson and Y^e Rampant Hare
Set out to find the HWOL;
They saw it in a murky pond
Behind a secret knoll.

A Naiad lived within the pond,
As happy as could be.
"I'll carry you into the HWOL
If you will marry me."

Then Lily swam into the dark;
Drake clutched fast to her skin.
And down he went, down far below;
The Second Key went in.

"Your steel is strong, my courtly knight,
But stronger still the sheath.
So kiss me long into the night,
And hold me underneath."

A White Horse shod with golden shoes
The next morn Drake did find.
His canter did Y^e Childe amuse,
With tail swishing behind.

"You need a steed, my courtly knight,
So climb up on my back.
And into Hell shall we take flight,
O noble son of Jack.

"And all I ask of you in turn,
A stable snug and warm."
"The deal is done," declared Y^e Owl.
They charged into the storm.

And down the muddy road he rode,
The sullen son of Jack,
Until he reached the Stygian bridge
From which may none turn back.

And there he found a Monkey bound,
Who shook his chains and cried,
"A Silver Key will set me free,
My hope has never died."

So Jackson kindly loosed his chains
And opened the Third Gate.
He broke the bonds which tie us all
And make men mock and hate.

Across the bridge there stopped a train;
Drake boarded it to ride.
He found a berth for Lily's bed
And lay himself beside.

A-rattling chains, the conductor
Possessed a skull-like head.
His body but a bag of bones,
He looked like he was dead.

"I ask of you my riddle's key,
And I have naught to hide;
Your answer will your ticket be
And pay me for your ride.

"O what is higher than a tree
And heavier than lead,
And what is deeper than the sea
And tastier than bread?

"And what is whiter than the milk
And sharper than a thorn,
And what is softer than the silk
And louder than a horn!"

And Jackson turned a Key to Hell
By how he made reply.
There was no sharper wit than he;
The son of Jack was sly.

"O heaven's higher than a tree,
And sin outweighs the lead,
And Hell is deeper than the sea,
And blessing outsweets bread.

"And snow is whiter than the milk,
And hunger outpricks thorn,
And down is softer than the silk,
And shame the loudest horn."

The train pulled into a bleak town
Called Tupelo by name.
They say that there a king was born,
A beggar all the same.

The rain fell down in Tupelo,
No welcome for them there,
No pillow for poor Jackson's head,
Or Lily or Y^e Hare.

No tavern's warmth or food or drink,
And jailed for vagrancy,
The monkey sprung them from the clink;
He jacked the sheriff's key.

Right quick they then did fly from town,
The sheriff on their trail.
The Duke boys hid them in a barn
And gave them beds and ale.

The rooster crowed the crack of dawn,
And coffee Drake was served.
He relished long his eggs and ham,
A breakfast well deserved.

Drake saddled up his sturdy horse
And galloped out of town.
He did his best to stay the course
While rain came pouring down.

And down the road a carny came;
A barker ran his mouth.
"Come see the spectacle!" he cried.
"The Wonder of the South.

48

"See He-She-Its arrayed in chains,
A horned three-headed freak,
Midget men and giant ladies,
You'll want to take a peek.

"Lion-tamers, fortune-tellers,
And oddities abound.
All tickets are a dollar, folks,
The cheapest show around."

Next to a shoestring puppet show
Childe Jackson met a girl.
She read his fortune with her cards;
He watched his fate unfurl.

His path was forked—so said her cards,
A spade on every one;
His father took the crooked path,
So straight must walk the son.

The rope which held the bigtop up
Was bound up in a knot
As twisted as a dragon's tail;
Untie it Drake could not.

And Satan said, "Who will untie
My twisty little ravel?
The crow will fly into the sky
When hammer strikes the gavel."

The Fifth Key turned into a sword
To cleave the knot in two,
And Satan fled, his purpose spurned;
Into the sky he flew.

That tent of blue they call the sky
Then came a-tumbling down;
A bat from hell, the carny flew,
Packed up and skipped the town.

A cockatrice, or basilisk,
Is hatched from basest dung,
And if you catch the merest glance
Your death knell will be rung.

A Billy Goat with flashing eyes
Asked Drake a deal be done.
"I'll carry you across the wall
If you give me a son."

"I'd scale that wall better'n no goat,"
The White Horse blurted out.
"Don't take that deal; climb on my back;
That bargain I will flout."

The Monkey caught yon Lurker's eye,
Averting so its gaze.
The White Horse then climbed up the wall;
His skill did all amaze.

He kicked the monster with his hooves.
Y^e Lurker then fell down,
Like Humpty Dumpty from the wall;
Its screams alarmed the town.

The Cockatrice cracked like an egg,
Its binding rune thus broke,
And as it shattered into bits,
The Sixth Gate so awoke.

Childe Jackson went where none return,
Where Lucifer await,
Y^e Lake of Fire where sinners burn,
Before him yawned the Gate.

A Court of Crows assembled there,
Asmodeus the Judge,
And Lucifer the Litigant,
Who held an age-old grudge.

A Boar defended Jackson Drake,
And ah, now here's the rub:
The prosecutor was the Goat,
Still smarting from the snub.

"Hear ye, hear ye," the Judge declared.
"The trial has now begun."
"How do you plead, Childe Jackson Drake,
Whom Jack once called his son?"

"A word of counsel," whispered the Boar.
"A truth that I have learned.
Whatever that is said in Court
Against you can be turned."

"How plead you?" the Judge asked him.
"To deals thy father struck?"
"I shall not pay for inborn sin,"
Said Drake to push his luck.

"Irrelevant," the Goat rebut,
The tone a haughty sneer.
"That Jack is bound and so his son,
The terms are crystal-clear."

"Who will stand witness," asked the Judge.
"To damn the Drake to Hell?"
And into Court an Angel flew,
His name was Azazel.

"I will," quoth he. "I saw the deed.
I witnessed well the deal.
"Jack signed his name with raven's quill,
And so his fate was sealed."

Then sauntered in a gold-haired Prince,
Lord Lucifer by name,
Who fell from grace and ever since
Has played a double game.

The court all rose for their fair King,
Whose locks steamed long behind;
Black ravens from their perch took wing,
Magnificent in kind.

The Daemon Prince a watch then pulled
From out of his silk vest.
The wheel of time did sorely put
His patience to the test.

He placed a hand upon a book,
And took the Oath of Wyrms:
"The truth and lies are both the same,
And none my oath confirms."

The Billy Goat did snort and champ.
"My client stakes his claim
To take the soul of Jackson Drake
As Jack he did the same."

Yᵉ Buke of Olde is bound in skin,
Where all of Time is found;
Two cherubim did crack it wide,
And in it Jack was bound.

"Fear not the deal, my dearest son;
I have your freedom here.
Your drink from Yᵉ White Cup is won;
Of Hell you have no fear."

The cherubs closed Y^e Olden Buke,
And in the Court did land
A seraph decked with beryl rings,
A letter in his hand.

"To Jackson Drake I offer you
A drink from Y^e White Cup
If you will come to me tonight
And join me in my sup."

"The deal is done," then screech'd Y^e Owl;
A reckoning was due.
The Seventh Gate swung open wide
For Jackson to pass through.

A soaring stair he found therein;
It spiralled up and up.
He climbed it till he huffed and puffed,
A-thirsting for Y^e Cup.

Atop the stair an ashen door,
As high as seven men.
He turned the Eighth Key in the lock;
It opened for him then.

Queen Lilith lay upon a bed,
A postered nest for one.
It was a rosy silken throne,
And he a Night had won.

The Queen set tea for Jackson Drake,
A pot of tea for two,
In china cups with silver spoons,
And honey in them too.

As Jackson quaffed his cup of tea,
Still reeling from the stairs,
He did not know until he had
The state of his affairs.

A gust of wind carried the Drake
Up from Y^e Mouth of Hell.
And borne aloft through the Ninth Gate,
He climbed up from a well.

He brushed the dust then off his tails,
The ash and soot and sand;
He found a stone, the Emerald,
A-glitt'ring in his hand.

He drank an ale at a tavern
That stood by crossing roads,
And left before the nighttime fell
And drunkards crooned their odes.

He paid his due to Oak and Ash,
Without forgetting Thorn;
And sighting home the heavens heard
Tantivy from his horn.

And in the hall a fire burned,
Awaiting him Y^e Hare;
They roasted chestnuts in the fire,
And all was well in there.

Zann

Ian Futter

It squeals and screeches
through the void;
ebullient screams,
and howls of joy.

His fingers fast,
on fretted boards,
twist from their joints
to chaos chords.

Strained notes through unknown octaves
spin
from resined bow
of cryptic skin,

an ancient air,
thrust through the years,
away from vapid, feeble ears.

Faster, faster
plays the fool.
The instrument with human tool.

Vast window,
open to the night,
like hungry maw,
receives his rite.

The Golden Diadem

Leigh Blackmore

I used to love to ride but then I fell;
They say I've never been the same since then.
Insane? No—prisoned in a desperate hell
In an asylum; yet I live to tell

The tale of Wilde, he of the yellow face,
Who fixed wrecked reputations on the sly.
His was a mystic, most mysterious case.
How many served him only but to die?

All waxen were his artificial ears;
He had no fingers on his crippled hand;
Yet from his lair he spread his special fears
Through city, state, and all the trembling land.

My name is Hildred Castaigne and I serve
The Yellow King whose cousin close I am;
The King whose story racks on every nerve,
Whose shadow haunts sane thoughts with curse and damn

Destruction. Emperors have served the King;
Dim hints survive of what he might portend;
But my ambition high to which I cling—
To take my rightful place, the world to mend.

The shadows gather in the fading light;
I don the white silk robe with Yellow Sign;
I well recall the awful words of fright
That echo through Carcosa's cursed line.

The diadem of diamonds and of gold
Is flashing fire—dare not tell me that
It is but bronze and paste! It is the crown
For which I suffered Wilde's demon cat!

Some say the author of the dreaded book
Had shot himself; we know that it was seized
In France by those who did not dare to look
Into its pages, lest it prove diseased.

Censured it was, denounced as devil's tool—
The King in Yellow, maddening supreme text
Of purest poison, writ to make men drool
And leer; stupendous art—yet some would call it hexed.

The scalloped tatters of the King must hide
The fearful memory of the Pallid Mask
Whose rule is coming; while Black Stars abide
Above the lake of Hali; the dread task

Is playing out to its stupendous end.
Infection-like, the book spreads despite pleas;
Some tried to burn it. Let the whole world bend
The knee—the King and Pallid Mask appease!

King in Carcosa I shall shortly be,
And King in Hastur where Camilla screams;
O'er Demhe and Yhtill from sea to sea;
My gaoler Archer's throat slit (in my dreams).

A Dynasty Carcosan lives on yet,
I bear that truth within my blood, each vein;
And though you lock me up, please don't forget
I bite and scratch you but I'm *not insane!*

To See or Not to See?

Nicole Cushing

I walk at night and see the King of Ghouls.
I swallow pills that make him abdicate.
And then I walk among the sane (the fools
who've never seen a wraith or fiend or Fate).
To see or not to see dark realms beyond
this place and time and halfwit humankind?
Oh madness, free me from the slavish bond
that makes me yearn to hold on to my mind!
They claim that, yes, I'm well, I'm cured, I'm whole
now that I see the world only in part.
But back and forth I go, unsure this goal
is fitting for this beast with Satan's heart.
In madness there is fear and pain and screams.
In sanity, no room for devil-dreams.

The Dark at the Top of the Stairs

Jonathan Thomas

Wait and see who dares
The dark at the top of the stairs.
All we know is something's wrong.
This house has stood empty so long.

The longer it's waited for someone to care,
The more people say that it's haunted in there,
But who used to live here and why they moved out
Are questions we don't know the first thing about.

Pause a while at the door,
Look out for the boards that were pried off the floor.
No more treasure to be found.
Do owls and wind make that sad midnight sound?

The longer it needs someone giving it love,
The more that its darkness will scare people off.
On the innermost soul, no one stops to reflect,
Is it wholesome or all eaten up with neglect?

Be careful as you go.
A step may give way to disaster below.
From above comes a sound.
Someone or something is moving around.

The longer you wait before going ahead,
The more that your feet seems as heavy as lead.
It feels just like déjà vu after a while.
Was this your worst nightmare when you were a child?

In the dark, start to see,
Something is waiting for you and for me.
Closing in as we draw near,
With an expressing inspiring fear.

It does what we do when we stop or we go,
As if we are mocked by a devil we know,
That turns out to be a reflection in glass,
While a voice in your head says you've come home at last.

Butterfly

Carole Abourjeili

For my friend, the artist

Raise mine earth to thy Demons' grave
Thy dusty tomb wherein I cave
Strum my pain thy deadly moon
Soothe my soul
Thy sweet *Qanoon*
Thus blessèd strings shall heal my pain
Mine interred earth shall rise again
Laud thy sins upon my breath
Thus I shall triumph a thousand deaths
Raise mine earth to thy Demons' grave
Thy dusty tomb wherein I cave

A *Qanoon* is string instrument, a type of large zither, mainly played in the middle east, Central Asia, and South Eastern Europe.

Weave thyself into my shell, then
Paint me, I prithee!
Blow thy breath to form my cells
Dwell in mine ecstasy
Thus I shall dance my love to thee
Lay in my finite sphere
A worm is *all* I am today
Yet tomorrow may disappear
Raise mine earth to thy Demons' grave
Thy dusty tomb wherein I cave

Sway thy hands upon my dust
Spill thy stains on my wound
Stroke thy brush thus quench my lust
Enchant my holy womb
Thus I command thy sinful reds
Onto my treacherous skies
Thus I compose thy saintly tunes
A thousand angel cries
Raise mine earth to thy Demons' grave
Thy dusty tomb wherein I cave

The beckoning hour, dear, hath come
Thy kiss of my first sun
Come hither, dwell into my soul
My shell hath become undone

This day hath come to crucify
Mine evil darkened state
Thus I shall conquer mine afterlife
With thy kiss to reincarnate
Raise mine earth to thy Demons' grave
Thy dusty tomb wherein I cave

Thy beaming sun hath lit my wings
I come to meet thy sky
Enthral thy soul within my sins
That I may haply die
I bid farewell, my love, to thee
For death waits at my door
I bid farewell, my love, to thee
For a worm I am no more
Thus I shall cleave my heart to thine
Thy beats shall multiply
Thus I shall whisper a thousand times
        ". . . Thy secret butterfly"
Raise mine earth to thy Demons' grave
Thy dusty tomb wherein I cave.

Carcosa in Mind

DJ Tyrer

Just a simple passing fancy
A word remembered from a play
Read once long ago
Yet insinuated deep
Within a layer of subconscious
Impossible to shift
Strangely supernal syllables
Tantalising the mind
Carcosa
City of soaring towers
Alien geometries
And fleeting shadows
Flickering in the corner of the eye
Of those wandering through that city
Carcosa

The Death of Twilight

D. L. Myers

Alone the ruddy leaves in Twilight's grasp
Sail high against the purple sky's dark coat
And paint the rising moon upon the clouds,
A jaundiced eye that foully stares and gloats.

A creeping ground-fog haunts the dying light
And furtive things peer from within its midst;
Disturbing faces drifting in the brume
With leprous, evil smiles that leer and twist.

All Hallow's Eve has come with Twilight's death
And witch-light blooms in every pumpkin maw;
Vile glimmers in the inky, spreading night
Where feral demons grope with tooth and claw.

Tragic, Trembling Giant

Linda D. Addison

Broken open, reality, a thin egg shell
between here and there, tastes
bitter, tastes sweet.

What is under your skin, is
under mine. We are I. The
illusion of separate exists
only in dreams.
    Wake up!

The collected one, waking to
the Truth. What is done to One
is done to All. Tears, blood mix.
Reminders that we own nothing,
    no one.

Each of us, a drop in the infinite
One. Star dust dance in our atoms,
part of The Orchestra. Time, a
dream. Space, a dream.
    Wake up!

Witches at the Switches

David Barker

Ghosts with tapers,
exuding vapors.
Ghouls draped in jewels.
Fiends clad in jeans.
Devils armed with bevels
and warlocks in frocks.
Witches at the switches,
sending trains into ditches.

At certain unknown vectors,
you'll encounter specters.
Beyond night's pale rim
the stars grow wan and dim.
Their feeble ancient gleaming
illuminates your dreaming.

Taunted and then haunted.
Glorified then horrified.
Disheveled and bedeviled.
Nuked and soon spooked.

Phantoms strut like bantams.
Vampires scale high spires.
Night-gaunts besiege cool haunts
bringing death with just one breath.

*   *   *

Flame-faced devils
lost in carnival revels.
Dog-faced ghouls
wielding razor-edged tools.
Carrion-breathed warlocks
bashing heads on flat rocks.
The blood they let is streaming
through your demon-tortured dreaming.

And in fungus-draped tombs
below abandoned rooms,
ultratelluric pentangles are
inscribed at eldritch angles,
while the crones lick the bones
of the snitches from the ditches.

My Heart's Thin Veil

Margi Curtis

Too often I have come to this dark place—
Moist grotto overgrown with summer's heat.
Too often I have hoped to see your face
Appear within the leaves, our eyes to meet,
For you to take my hand, and take the lead,
Draw me on down to faery, where I'm freed.

I come this night at dusk. I am between,
Upon the edge of dream, of life and death.
Faint scent is heavy on cool airs unseen.
My hair stirs nonetheless. Is this your breath?
I quell the urge to turn, remaining still
Lest I might break a spell you could fulfil.

My heart is pounding now, I dare not move,
Though custom would dictate an offering
(Placed thoughtfully just so, with care and love)
Might please reluctant fae still lingering,
Someone of you perchance, who might look back
Between the Worlds, before you close the crack.

A melody, a hum, a sound of play
Escapes my lips. My empty hands extend.
This song is all I have to give you, fae.

No part of me can tell what you intend,
Suspended as I am 'twixt day and night:
Reality's harsh glare or dark delight.

A sudden gust of wind whips through the trees.
My neck and cheek receive a brief caress.
I start and spin, caught up in fronds and leaves,
And fall down backward, tangled in a mess.
From out the earth I hear wild laughter ring
While insects, birds and frogs begin to sing.

I realise I have no privilege dear.
You dance with every creature through the green.
I am but one of many who come here
To sing in courtship of their faery queen.
When I return again I vow to make
A song to touch your heart—lest my heart break.

Clarethea

K. A. Opperman

As I survey this violet-misted vale
From this my castle in Carpathia,
I think of only my Clarethea,
Who in despair leapt from this balcon-rail.

The wolves that howl within the woods below
Raise for Clarethea their canine rune—
Nay, nevermore unto the wan full moon
Shall they address their wild and ancient woe!

I watch the phantom of her funeral
Procession pass along the lonely road;
They bear Clarethea to death's abode;
Their torches flare in twilight mystical.

This very eve it was, a twelvemonth flown,
That my Clarethea was laid to rest
In her ancestral tomb—the storied nest
Of deathless vampires, as we well had known.

She often haunts this crumbling balcony,
The pallid specter of Clarethea;
And when the sun sets on Carpathia,
Will I await her, freed from misery.

Whether my love, or devil, on this eve
I go to be with her forevermore—
Clarethea! love whom I most adore!
For you all life and light I fain would leave.

I hear the distant tolling of the bell
The village chapel rings at vesper-time—
For fair Clarethea they sound the chime,
And for my death they sound the doomful knell.

This is my final sunset, this, my last,
And ever after, the eternal night.
Clarethea! my bride, my starry-bright!
We are together in the golden past.

Ghoul of the Enamel

Jason Sturner

Tonight we sense him, hiding in the sunken shadows of the bedroom: a ghoul creeping silent, forcing quiet the other monsters. Chunks of enamel, grooved by nightly gnawing, fatten his belly. And our own teeth tighten in the jaw, fight the urge to drop and slip away, to escape his gluttonous rage. You see, the foul thing broke from fairy law: took to ripping out the loose teeth of children, a calcareous shit slipped beneath their bloodied pillows in a gesture of defiance; a jab at us proper fairies. And though imprisoned for a time in the amber caves, he broke free— saber arms flapping and chipping with madness.

Now we wait within this toy-box, scanning the room for residual energies: the moans of bloody roots, the chattering of crowns, the hissing red of severed nerves . . . Such things betray his whereabouts.

At last we fly and crawl from the moonlit box, our eyes narrowed and our tongues writhing with an invocation. How swift, how sweet the coming of revenge from its ancient lair! Soon the children will sleep soundly; none will recall the ghoul's attack. Money will distribute where due, and the status of the tooth fairy will once again be restored to its innocuous state. Because tonight we are going to pounce on the fiend. Unravel his existence. Shred into his stomach and take back what is ours.

A Queen in Hell

Ashley Dioses

To Edgar Allan Poe

Upon a moonlit eve, we strolled along the shores
Of a still lake, all atrament save for the bright,
Rich, hoary moon-glow, which threw wide dark, eldritch doors
Into a hell of reeking hells that stole her light.

My love, my gorgeous love, how could you abandon me?
What haunting daemons lured you to your early grave?
How could you not perceive that you were always free?
Why, why was it not you, my love, that I could save?

The years have passed and sadly I stand so alone
Beside you, by your grave, yet in my heart you dwell.
Your kinsmen knew of your great beauty, and it's known
That we lament so deeply for a queen in Hell.

Azathoth

Charles Lovecraft

A dream's malignant locus in my head
Foretold the end of all things known. The talk
On loud, annoying radios, would squawk
In horrible sound bytes. My dead ears bled,
Filling with suppuration my bleared mind,
As if some marsh had leaked its filthy damp
Into the chasms of my being, black swamp
That I could never shake from its dark bind.

But Azathoth had come some said, and prayed
To all their gods, and the whole Earth grew hot
Like some mad magnifier burned our spot
From realms beyond all time, and source betrayed.
    Atomic chaos seared all life like some
    Summer of love—save that its love was doom.

Waking

Ian Futter

Some of my demons ascend
In the day;
bright, withering light-mares.
Fresh from the pit, caked in sulphur
and clay;
shock, shimmering sun-scares.

Most of my demons will sleep
through the dark,
In tune with my heart's breath.
Beneath my closed lids, in the id,
these soul sharks
will swim up from the dream's death.

All my demons, on waking,
will taunt,
Compressing my thoughts, tight.
With panic primed pressure and fear
they will haunt.
I long for the long night.

Spinal Piano

Reiss McGuinness

The last wave on her back has broken.
The segment of spine that jutted out
like a rib on an emaciated chest
has popped, pushing the skin of her back up.
Then the rest of her spine goes.

It is as if each vertebra is a piano hammer stringed to keys,
and a pianist is walking his fingers across the notes,
pulling each vertebra up one by one
till her back is as rugged and red as a sore elbow.

Each spinal hammer is held down to elongate the note,
lengthen her screams of pain.
The longer they press up against her back the tighter,
redder, more pointed the skin becomes.

Then her skin comes off,
like a bed sheet pulled too tight at one end,
it pulls out the recently tucked in edge at the other end,
but, rather than a muted bump as the cloth comes untucked,
the sound of tearing wallpaper in two
screeches through the air, as the force of her spine being pulled
tears open her skin in a perfect line from her hip to armpit,
and I pull the loose skin back.

Her now exposed, skinned back: the red muscle,
the white ribs pulled into the punctured lungs,
the beating heart, the throbbing gristle,
the shiny meatiness of it on display.

She performs her last writings as the damp spinal cord tears in two
like a wet cardboard cylinder filled with dishwater,
and then, as if the pianist released his fingers,
each vertebra falls back into place at once, spinal chord closes,
and the threads of her back reseal the exposed flesh,
and I tie them, like threading a corset,
each knot is tight so her skin does not sag, her organs hold,
until the next shifting performance.
I kiss her on the back goodnight.

The Thirst of Sekhmet

Ann K. Schwader

There is a crying on this twilight wind
Like some great lioness who scents the blood
Of Aegypt spilled afresh: that primal flood
Re once unleashed. Just how the people sinned
Against their god is lost, but his reply
Clawed swift in hieroglyphs of solar fire
Across men's hearts, translating his desire
For retribution through his daughter. Eye
Of vengeance merciless as midday heat,
She hunted & she slaughtered & she bled
Fresh sacrifice enough to wade in red,
Until Re formulated her retreat.

All this is myth; yet myths may still awake
When offered what they crave. The taste of fear
Is salt & copper, spreading like a stain
Across the ravaged land once more to slake
Its first & fiercest rage . . . for it was here
A goddess thirsted. And shall thirst again.

The Shadow within Darkness

Randall Larson

Blackness in shadow.
An inky presence discerned
Dark limbs scrape night air.

Shadow in the void.
Darkness beyond ebony
Roiling out at me.

Black liquid tendrils
Snap out, grasp my face, pull me
into the dark void

And all is blackness.
Absorbed by the black chasm,
my being dissolves

Guardians of the Seven Gates

Chad Hensley

I. The Skeleton King

A frost giant's skull is fused to the spine
Of Skeleton King's barbarian bones.
Fleshless fingers grasp a labrys of chine,
Back hunched as it stands waiting and bemoans

How it came to guard the first gate of Hell,
Thoughts of berserkers battling eternally.
Or is the result of a wizard's spell,
Knowing it will live on permanently

Or be defeated by a mortal sword
Its hunger depleted for human blood.
Then six gates stand against the demon horde
Yet it wonders if death will be a thud

Or a great bellow when the first gate falls
The hot wind filled with the tyrants' catcalls.

II. The Arch Goat

The Arch Goat guards the second gate of Hell
Standing upon enormous hoofed hind legs.
Huge membranous black wings flap a death knell
Urinating vile, oily boiling dregs

What it ate with its mouth of saber teeth.
Its swollen human hands hold a great whip
While it's curved goat horns wear a thorn wreath
That tear tiny wounds of green blood that drip

Down its buck face into over-sized eyes
That glare with pure ferocious, feral hate.
It lusts to fight and kill until its demise
All that attempt to pass through the gate.

Yet even it knows a day will arise
When it shall fall to the earth as it dies.

Schadenfreude

John Mundy

The painting mocked him.
The very light of the studio seemed tainted,
Darkened and poisoned with his failure.
How many times must he repeat
These scenes of disappointment and madness?
He had tried to infuse a canvas with Life
A *perfect* representation of the cruel inspirations
That writhed and coiled about his sleeping brain;
The horrors that stained his meager cot with cold sweat.
O, to rid himself of those images that tormented his nights,
Those shapes of nightmare that filled his dreams!
One dim hope had guided the artist's every brush stroke:
The certainty that an *artistic triumph* could be his liberation;
For surely, he reasoned, if desire *commands* its own extinction
The stilling of the compulsion to give Life
To such vile images of icy horror
Might stifle forever the source!
In the end his talents had failed him
A *perfect* living work of art was beyond his reach.
And now one more failure to be dealt with
Before beginning his mad work anew . . .
Cursing, he grasped the palate knife
And slashed savagely at the botched canvas,
Screaming mindlessly at Its travesty,
Relenting only when It could no longer scream back.

Dead Pale Moon

(for Nora May French)

Leigh Blackmore

Bright day is done with all its work of gleaming,
And vanished now the dewdrops crystal-seeming;
Dim forest depths grow steeped in dusky glooms;
The flowers gold and green close all their blooms.

The placid pool, draped 'round by weeping willows,
Is rippled by chill winds' uprising billows—
Serene no more. The rains send silver ringing
Upon black earth as startled birds go winging.

The crimson kiss of sunset now subsiding
Lends twilight's arch a bloody tinge abiding
And all day's woven, wondrous, lustrous threads
Flee glimmering and surging, torn in shreds.

Now creep the blacks and purples slowly shifting
'Neath spectral silent Maiden whitely lifting.
Can face so pocked and leering prove a boon?
Fall to your knees before the dead pale Moon!

To Reach Carcosa

Mark McLaughlin

Carcosa can be reached in many ways,
but you won't find the route on any map.
For some, the trip takes countless stormy days,
while others make the journey in a snap.
Some seek the wisdom of the Yellow King,
not knowing of the venom in His words.
Some simply wish to hear Cassilda sing,
accompanied by gleaming silver birds.
You think you'd like to go there? Think some more.
You really must forget this foolish goal.
You claim your life is such a dreary bore—
but boredom will not jeopardize your soul.
You want the truth, my friend? This I shall tell:
To reach Carcosa, one must pass through Hell.

Sand Bar

Jonathan Thomas

On that lonely stretch of beach at dawn,
The gulls are crying and fog comes on.
There's decay in the air as the tide gets low
And a sand bar like bone begins to show.

You can travel so far when the tide ebbs away
As if on a road halfway into the bay,
And clues come to light as the fog closes in
Why they say that the sand hides uncountable sins.

Sometimes you and I are exposed that way,
Strange discoveries under the everyday.
But spend too much time out upon that limb,
You may well be drowned when the tide rushes in.

Who can tell if disaster had taken a hand
In those things that you find all but buried in sand?
An overturned rowboat or some clothing in shreds,
What might be an arm but it's driftwood instead.

Then you feel the tide rising and turn back at last,
Where the water around you seems deep as the past.
Keep your feet on the path or you'll be out of luck.
Things with stingers and claws come awake in the muck.

Toujours Il Coûte Trop Cher

Mike Allen and C. S. E. Cooney

"In the time of Shakespeare, Joan of Arc was accepted in England as a symbol for everything vile. He makes her out not only as a sorceress, but a charlatan and a hypocrite; and on top of that a coward, a liar and a common slut. I suspect they began to whitewash her when they decided that she was a virgin, that is a sexually deranged, or at least incomplete, animal, but the idea has always got people going, as any student of religion knows. Anyway, her stock went up to the point of canonization. Gilles de Rais, on the other hand, is equally a household word for monstrous vices and crimes. So much so, that he is even confused with the fabulous figure of Bluebeard, of whom, even were he real, we know nothing much beyond that he reacted in the most manly way to the problem of domestic infelicity. . . . I think, then, it is not altogether unfair to assume that Gilles de Rais was to a large extent the victim of Catholic logic. Catholic logic: and the foul wish-phantasms generated of its repressions, and of its fear and ignorance. He wanted to confer a boon on humanity; therefore he consorted with the learned; therefore he murdered little children."

—Aleister Crowley

1. GILLES

Once I slept on satin. Now it's rat shit and straw,
goose-down pillows now piss-stained stone.
They told me they'd hang me from hooks if I didn't
confess to those lies, confess to dangling those boys,
strangling those boys, slitting those boys

and pulling out their innards, treating them as toys,
making them watch as I pulled them apart,
sitting on their stomachs and turning them blue,
watching veins bulge and burst as I . . . as I . . . as I . . .
but none of it true! None of it! None! I am no sadist, no Satanist,
no pederast, I am none of these things, I am favored
of the King, Marshall of France, I have spilled the blood of filthy
        islanders
across mile after mile to restore the glory of the throne!
But they thrust prongs and heated tongs in my face,
told me, move my tongue or die without one,
promised torture me if I did not admit torture,
pledged to sever my soul from Heaven if I did not give the Church
the false perversions it demanded. The Bishop, in his greed,
wants my manse, my lands, my title deeds, and if I must lose them, let it be!
But You, whose light, whose holy glow is surely that
I see through the slat in this forsaken door,
You must know what truth beats in my heart,
which will drop with me through the trap door in the morn
and snap when my neck cracks from my shoulders. Yes, You.
This light that shows me every granule of dust in this cell
could never come from the moon, not down here, not so removed.
O, Father, if it is You, grant miracles, spring the lock,
or grant me last sleep and escape to Paradise!
Let this luster be the last I ever see in this place!

2. JEANNE

Chevalier, at ease! The Maid is here, your Jeanne
your friend, it's been too many years, monsieur.
Your beard is long, your skin is loose, you smell as rank as I did
 after weeks in Vermandois. But never mind!
How sweet to see you, looking up at me like that, as if I were
a light, a torch, a corpse burned thrice to prove my heresy—but pardon me—
of course you were not there! One forgets.
Do you regret those days, Chevalier? Or did you cast my memory
like ash into the Seine? I've heard so much about you in the interim:
alchemy, sodomy, theatrical productions, an attempt or more to raise
a demon, and now—your own execution! Another thing we have in
        common.
Is it comfort you seek, my comrade, my companion in arms?
Absolution? Veneration? Shall I kiss these weeping holes that
yesterday were fingernails, these wounds that bled confession
to deeds so dark they must be writ in blood?
Shall I change your sores to jewels, promise you a life eternal
at my side, beneath my banner, haloed, holy
with cherubim to diddle daily while seraphic fiddlers play?
Is this what you wish from me, Gilles de Rais?

3. GILLES

What mad sorcery curls its fumes before my eyes?
This light you wear, it shines, swims behind your skin,
your face a lantern . . . you shimmer like a stained glass saint,
which you, crazed witch, could no more be than I
Lord of the Fairie Mounds. No Christian prayer of mine
could draw *you* as an answer. For damned Jeanne,
no Resurrection! This is no alchemy, no silly piddling
in fool's gold, this is evil beyond measure—Father,
O, Father, sweep aside this creature,
this luminescent shade of a madwoman . . .
Fraud in life and death! Fell devils spoke in many tongues
on the stage of your broken mind, their fervor stoking that glow
so magnetizing in your eyes, but it was my lone voice
won your campaigns. One more whisper in your head
but this one in your ear, to direct a mind pliant as butter.
Those armies behind you, gullible men eager for divine favor,
but it was I that engineered all your battlefield glory.

Father! Hear me! I have always been Your hand.
My blade drank soldiers, not children, emptied only deserving men
and more deserving cowards. I know no angel stands before me.
Tis a last wile of that heinous bishop, to send
this Jeanne in effigy, blazing brighter than she did even in death.
This cannot be a thing of yours, Lord. Make it not be!

4. JEANNE

I cry your pardon, cher seigneur!
Of course *you* know what's holy, what is pure,
you who've muttered all the Mass of Saint Sécaire
from aft to fore, who've drunk deep of the waters
of the drowned, and lit your aloes and your incense
in a dead man's skull, until the black glass bell
of midnight rang, and ringing woke the angels from their dreams of hell.
You're the expert on the sacrosanct—no prince or priest
or half-baked prophet girl revivified from death
would dare deny it—why, Christ Himself has often pined to
transubstantiate His little toe into a sou, and with it pay
admission to your passion plays, those revelries
that rival paradise: what, again, your asking price?
A peasant boy, perhaps, so pretty, flushed and tender
 crying *kyrie eleison* in shrill soprano splendor?
You shudder now. Can it be you don't remember?
Strange what we neglect in pious self-reflection,
what truths we conjure or discard at whim
naked in the light by which all other lights grow dim.
But shade or demon, Bride of Satan, Queen of Heaven
here I stand, sole witness to your last confession.
Therefore, Chevalier, my saintly Gilles de Rais
Speak on! For it is almost dawn.

5. GILLES

You corrupt creature! Baffle my eyes with radiance,
with every perfect-mimicked manner, yet I say again,
you cannot be Heaven-sent, for no thing divine could open lips
and spew those vomitous lies with such aching-sweet smiles,
speak with such moist sadness as you spin mockeries, the greatest of these
your usurpation of a simple girl's face. You exist
in my delusions, it must be so, else you're another trick,
I'm sure, a last ploy of the bishops to absolve their own black guilts
over the vile untruths they have twisted from my throat.
I deny their false power. You are not there. You are illusion.
As are all these movements you conjure in the shadows,
all mere figment, these crawling limbs, fleeting mirage.
The walls do not seethe with spidery and shriveled cherubim.
They are not there. No eyeless youth plays cat's-cradle
with his own entrails in the corner. The floor is not smothered
with faces, baby-fat faces turning black as they wheeze
for breath. These cruel giggles that echo, those disgusting
 moans of ecstasy, that is not my own voice, it—is—not. *It is not.*
Those smells, seeping, septic—that taste—what is this—
on my tongue? Lord. My God. Stop this! I pray—Strip away
these traitor senses! Father. Father! Father! Save me!

6. JEANNE

All right! Enough, I say! Stop gibbering! Really, Gilles,
a man like you, of influence, ignominy—aren't you ashamed?
How you do groan and foam and slobber—oh, don't start up again, you
     hypocrite,
 apostate, puppet, shrieking *Father, take this cup from me!*
As if you were the Star of Morning!
No, you're right, you're absolutely right, I'm not your girl, the Maid of Orleans
your Jeanne—she's gone, she's atomized, at one with all the universe, and she
shall be a saint famed the whole world over.
Young damsels swinging wooden swords will hope her tongue of flame
will render them important. But for you, my doomed one, a different
     myth shall bloom:
dark of root, ruin for its fruit
Young girls will whisper when they speak of you: they'll say your beard
     was blue
Yes, and how you snuffed a new wife every night and never knew contrition.
All the little boys who swarm your rotten robes will vanish, like their very
     bodies vanished
into cesspits, into ovens, into cellars, into ditches, the obscurity of history
shall erase them and replace them with a story and a moral, so delicious, Gilles!
So refreshing, Gilles! This reminds me I must thank you.
After centuries of boredom, no one living who remembered me
I wandered regions waterless and galaxies afar
Then, unlikely as an angel in an abattoir, sweet summons! You called. I came.

Some dabbler, some amateur, stumbling inebriate on mysteries beyond
  his grasp
You thought your tainted rituals as empty as your prayers
To lift you up in your despair, or just to lift you up in general—a
  problem, I recall.
A game. A spoilt child's game. But such a game!

Oh, Gilles, why do you scream so? You should love this kind of play.
These kinds of playmates. Just a sample, just a taste, in the dark before sunrise,
of what awaits when the rope takes all your light away.
How I hate to leave you, Gilles, but dawn is breaking, night is ending
Now the pigs to trough, the birds to branch, the king to his levee
Now the soldier must march forth, face the shadows of the gallows
face the gibbet, face his Maker, make his *peace*—

How sweet your face, suffused with hope at idle words,
how trusting, how absurd! Such delight you'll be
down there in the dark with me, for eons, for eternity, for however long
your torment stills my wanderlust, distracts and entertains—
but at last, Chevalier, my attention drifts,
my light withdraws. I, too, forget. I'll wander on
while you and all your broken screams remain.

> *Voyez, regardez, Cieux! L'échafaud, c'est le monde,*
> *Je suis le bourreau sombre, et j'exécute Dieu.*
>   —Victor Hugo

Alone in the Desert

Mary Krawczak Wilson

The falcon spies the skeletal remains
Of the lone man who crossed the Kalahari;
He sought shade beneath a baobob tree
And now the sun sears his skull, blood-stained.

A Bedouin devours the dates
Left lying in the desert space
Where he once laid to waste,
Sacrificing himself to an unknown fate.

An intrepid soul with no allegiance,
He dared answer an ethereal voice
And followed the echo without remorse;
He was swept up in sands—mystic and immense.

No one hears the raw rattling wind
As it scatters the antediluvian dust
Like kernels of corn on a dried-out husk;
It buries the skull inside the shimmering scrim.

Mother

Christina Sng

There were stars in her eyes,
Red dwarfs, filled with
The purest elements and life,
So vibrant, exuberant,
She filled with pride, breathless
From the joy she felt inside
Watching them thrive, multiply.

And then they changed,
They began to destroy.
These grievous angels she made
From her own loins. Now
Turned destructive and brutal.
Creatures gone wrong
Since their birth, their inception.

She loved and loathed them.
A mother's conundrum:
How to deal with the monsters
They had become. She sent
Fire and frost, but yet they
Endured. Finally she turned them
All to salt, and let them fertilize

The scorched earth once more.

The Perfect Rose

(To Nora May French)

Ashley Dioses

The soft and languid rays of dawn,
Of colors red and gold,
Caress the rose to which they're drawn,
A splendor to behold.

The silken petals painted red,
A scarlet like her lips,
Gleam out amid the poppy bed,
And shine till daylight slips.

The perfect rose, still young and pure,
Still timeless like a swan,
Can heed the storm and its strong lure—
It bloomed, and now is gone.

End Times

DJ Tyrer

The inadvertent recitation of a litany
Fulfilled that half-formed prophecy
Which the Mad Arab spoke centuries ago
Propelled by mighty cosmic forces
The stars were shifted in their courses
In an eldritch galactic light show
From the waters a lost land appeared
A city that held all man rightly feared
A myriad secrets man wasn't meant to know

The Lich's Last Laugh

Dan Clore

The wizard had sworn that he would resurrect the love of his youth, lost to a wasting disease that led her to an early tomb. He had spent decades studying abstruse tomes and grimoires, learning the mysteries of magick in order to repair his loss. He had mastered ever more powerful spells, but his excursions into the field of necromancy taught him only that the dead die utterly, leaving nothing to return or restore to life. Meanwhile, his friends and family had become a trail of corpses left in his wake as he himself became old and frail and knew that the final terminus soon awaited him.

And so the wizard swore that even if he could not raise the dead, at least he would not yield himself to Death's allure. And so he hurled himself back into the study of magick. He prepared his body with potions brewed under starlight from rare spices and wild herbs, until he finally swallowed a draught of poison that no mortal could survive—and he sat back and waited.

After what seemed eternities of struggle in the embrace of Death, falling in free flight down endless unlighted caverns, through sheer force of Will the wizard broke his enemy's hold and cast him aside. He found himself in his body once more; but as his eyes lit with a gleam that illuminated the vast central chamber of his ebon tower from his throne, he discovered that he could not move so much as the least thew or sinew of the stiff lich that sat motionless, desiccated and mummified, no matter how great the strength of Will he summoned—not even with the strength of a Will that could defeat Death itself. The lich contemplated its situation for ages, reflecting upon it as if through the maze of mirrors that was its immobile brain, and finally, just when it believed it had gone mad from the ineluctable irony, it burst aloud with a sinister chuckle that rattled the dust from the otherwise unmovable cadaver.

Over centuries that turned into millennia, the lich remained enthroned in its ebon tower, dreaming that it was not mad. Decades passed before anyone dared to disturb the guards and wards the wizard had placed about his lair. Then, a pair of tomb-robbers of unusual audacity and disrespect for superstition restrained their courage until they reached the great central chamber, and confronted the wizard still upright on his throne after all those many years—eyes burning and glowering face giving way to an evil, ironic laugh that sent the thieves in mad flight to the nearest town to spread legends of how the lich had leapt from its seat, strangled their third companion in crime, and how fortunate they had been to escape the effects of the *maranatha anathema* that it had pronounced upon them. And so few others had the bravery to make the attempt; but every few generations a similar story would recur, and so the lich laughed to itself at the fools too frightened to rob it of objects it could never use.

And so, after millennia of gathering dust only to shake it off occasionally with a laugh of monstrous irony as it beheld the backs of fleeing tomb-robbers through the motes as they settled in the beams of its eyes, the lich felt the ground beneath it shake. Not as the mild earthquakes that had damaged the structure before, leaving the tower in ruins about it, but such a quake as ended with the land beneath it sinking under the waves until the lich's eyes provided the only light to the occasional octopus who would shelter under its throne and examine it with curiosity as it burbled with irony. Further millennia passed before the lands shifted once again, and the seabed rose above the waves once again.

When tomb-robbers finally came again, they were of a different sort than in former times. They put no stock in superstitions; and when they perceived the uniquely well-preserved mummy and saw its glowing eyes and heard its strange laughter, they took the lich itself and placed it on display before gawking crowds as a relic of a bygone, barbaric age. Guides would describe how savants had explained the odd phosphorescence that the mummy's eyes had obtained during its long stay under the sea, and the internal mechanics that produced a crepitation remarkably similar in sound to an ironic chuckle—which the lich seemed to make as if on cue at this point in the lecture, causing many skeptics among the audience to believe the lich a fraud. But the civilization of these people did not last long before they had used their science against each other and a universal holocaust had turned the museum that housed the lich into ashes.

After this brief interlude of civilization humanity returned to its normal, more superstitious state, and a primitive tribe soon discovered the mummy and placed it high atop a frozen mountain peak. Their wisest shamans would make quests to consult the lich on the oddest, most esoteric matters, posing their queries in broken verse, and interpreting its single, unique chuckle according to their own lights, returning to their tribes to astonish their listeners with the latest revelations of the gods by way of their chosen messenger, and ordain ostracism and outlawry on any who clung to the older faith. Over the millennia, these shamans would visit less and less frequently, until the lich laughed with the surmise that there would be no more visits.

And after æons and æons of non-event in which the stars and sun collapsed into ashes and the lich's glowing eyes provided the graveyard of the universe with its last glimmer of unseen light, a final, cackling chuckle of irony arose in the wizards throat, beginning with a gurgle that rose higher and higher, bursting out of the lich's sepulchral oral cavity and echoing and reverberating in the universal nothingness, shaking and shattering the lich's body and brain until it crumbled and dissolved and mated with ultimate darkness and dust.

A Garden of Unearthly Delights

Marge Simon

after H. Bosch

I knew I'd find you here,
the residential haunt
of a dreary farmhouse
on the outskirts of Antwerp.
It had to be none other
for a medieval artesian,
Maestro of the Grotesque.

The sound of my footsteps
turns into hideous laughter
that whispers through the house
and will not die.

Eyes alight with green flames,
you appear in a filthy robe
to invite me to another world
where owls nest in the grass,
moons howl and trees have eyes.

You give it raucous music,
beacons lit by weeping violins
and flames to punctuate the sky.
Indeed, you've landscaped Hell,
outdone the most aesthetic demon
at the Dark Angel's command.

I've seen enough, I try to turn away,
but by some monstrous force, you intervene.
As my torch expires, I join your visions,
imprisoned in a baroque frame.

Masque Macabre

K. A. Opperman

Though I be dead, a body in the ground,
A putrid corpse imprisoned in this cask,
Yet I will dance at my beloved's masque,
Once more to view her gorgeously engowned.

For on this night of Halloween, the dead
Awake and walk beneath October's moon. . . .
O heart that beats defying death's black swoon,
Soon we will quit this sable satin bed. . . .

A crimson plague-mask and a matching cloak
Will serve to veil the dreadful form of death;
A crown of roses, herbs of healthful breath,
Will mask the stench till midnight's fateful stroke.

Thus will I dance away that dreamful night
With my beloved, in one timeless waltz,
Recalling romance from evanished vaults
That Time had shut forever in his flight.

The orchestra with rich, nocturnal airs,
Will lavish us with song of violins,
And all the masquers, costumed like strange sins,
Will watch us with grotesque, fantastic stares. . . .

But ere the clock strike twelve I must depart,
Slipping betwixt the scarlet drapes, unseen,
Into the night, unkissed by my One Queen—
For at that hour, my corpse must drag my heart

Back to the grave to pass a twelvemonth more
Pining for her, imprisoned, in the dark.
—I only hope her mourning heart will mark
A passing shadow from the days of yore.

Gorgoneion

Oliver Smith

A mirrored serpent slides through incandescent
Sunlight flaunting green-jewelled skin,
Flashing the midnight glitter of her eyes.
In her golden tongue she whispers
Sibilant eroticisms
To the petrified flesh that waits
Buried stone under stone.

An instrument sharp as a snake's tooth engraved
The meandering ornament; chiselled labyrinths
Interlocked into metamorphic stone.
Some flow left an evil accretion;
Suspicious stains on the marble;
Soiled, tarnished, blemished, and bloodstained.
One trespasser peeped in

Among these perfect statues in the garden overgrown
With roses; roses bred white as bone, bred red as blood;
Roses bred yellow as sins warm butter sunshine.
The curious remain,
Remembered as funereal effigies,
Stone in silence beneath the rose.
Metamorphic lips tight closed;

Motionless under deep green ivy and yielding moss.
He could not stop himself glancing into the casket
At her face as radiant as winter moonlight;
Her smile spreading as bright as a blood flow
And more fatal than scorpion stings,
Curare, cement, and the metamorphosis
Effected by passing time.

In the mirror that sly smile had once pleased him.
Her eyes were star-dark and lustrous
And her hair still shivered lush as springs
Shimmering venom-green.
But in the flesh she chilled like arctic night.
Now in the heart of her silent grove,
Her lover's memory grows cold.

On the overripe fleshiness of her purpled lips
Hangs the sleepy taste of asphodel and poppies;
Keys that unlock this tendrilled garden
Where she apprehends all her would-bes;
Lovers like belemnites, crinoids,
Urchins, ammonites: frozen hearts
And wormwood-bitter kisses.

Unexpected Meetings

Ian Futter

The first time he came
I was six;
a hammer, a tent,
and a wicked child's tricks.

A baseball bat exit
at nine;
a friend's faultless swing
and *his* shove, from behind.

I scratched his black car
at eleven.
A sharp shunt to the spine,
but no taxi to heaven.

Then I'm twenty
and losing my breath,
when for thirty-six hours
I'd been punching at death.

All my knuckles were splintered
with bones,
but still he smiled on
through my lungs'
gasping tones.

Since then,
when my heart hammers hard,
my bright blankets blaze black
through the nightly façade.

Maybe one day
this fear will withdraw,
In some hospital bed,
or passed out
on the floor.

On that day all chance meetings
will end,
and I'll greet *his* cold skull
as the smile of a friend.

Black Panther

David Barker

He traveled all day by foot, never once encountering anyone. His route took him through a wild region of dry, sparsely vegetated hills and arroyos filled with boulders. Scanning the horizon from each summit, he surveyed only further ranges and canyons. The abandoned mission was said to be sited in this country, although none had seen it for over a century. Rumors told of a crumbling ruin where once a noble structure had stood—a relic fallen prey to the depredations of relentless sun, encroaching nature, and the haunting spirits of its former occupants, the humble, hard-working fathers. Legend called it "The Lost Mission," for none knew its exact location, but some said the name actually implied "lost to the devil." Monsignor inspired fear among his flock; none dare oppose that fierce being. Some claimed a phantasmal beast, a giant cat of the hills, ever guarded the priestly wardrobe, lest some foolish thief purloin the Master's cloak. Late in the day the traveler found the antiquated edifice, its adobe walls yet erect but the ceiling decayed and in danger of collapse. The pews were all stripped out, pillaged by scavengers. With no candle to light his way, the interior was shroud in shadow and given over to spiders. Cobwebs hung in eerie drapery from the upper vaults. A coating of pigeon dung whitened the floor tiles. The air stank of age and decay. His treading raised motes that danced in the glow around gaping doors and windows. Exploring the depths, he surmised the looting had been complete. Until, that is, he came upon the cabinet of antique liturgical vestments. These were untouched; superstition played a role in their survival. Removing them one by one, turning each robe this way and that to catch the rays of failing light, he

came upon rich brocades and delicate embroideries. Silk and velvet shot
with gold thread, these garments were fashioned from the discarded
finery of courtly ladies who made of their cast-off gowns gifts to clothe
the monks. Each vesture more colorful than the last—reds, yellows,
purples. He thought to take them all away, the lot too lovely for the rats
and moths. But then he came to that unholy relic: the green robe worn
by the great Monsignor himself, the one some whispered was beholden
to demons. Simpler in design than the others—for Monsignor pretended
at humility—and heavily frayed from many years' use, the man's very
essence clung to this vestment. This one garment the traveler folded with
care, for it was precious—a terrible artifact from a powerful being.
Closing the cabinet—the other items returned to their pegs—he made to
leave, the bundle under his arm. Just then, he spied two eyes across the
dark chamber. Hot coals of fierce intent, glaring at him and the stolen
relic. Stolen? From whom? The ghost of a long dead padre? Or, from the
Church itself, a spiritual force even now in its sad ruination? The eyes
demanded he restore the vestment to its place. They darted left and
right. He imagined a ripple of satiny sinew, like wet tar against the night
sky—a glistening ebony form, shifting in the darkness. Stalking him? A
raw terror such as he had never known seized his limbs, holding him,
then releasing; he bolted for the door, sure he would feel an
overwhelming blow when that awesome predator pounced, ripping his
flesh to crimson shreds. Certainly, the hammering of his heart would kill
him, but it didn't, and with hot breath on his neck he burst from the
mission and fled that unmapped site—ran until his legs gave out,

collapsing on a hillside, the bundle clutched to his heaving chest. The beast did not follow; he was free, or so he thought. Walking most of the night, he escaped the accursed region. At dawn's glimmering, the traveler reached home. His heart swelled with greed, proud of this possession. But there was no joy in the owning. For on hot summer nights, when he awakens from fevered visions of a lost mission that no man has entered for more than a century, he sees on the dark balcony two widely spaced eyes—accusing orbs, burning coals of eternal hate—the eyes of the panther.

Classic Reprints

Old Trinity Churchard

A. Merritt

A lonely graveyard lies between high walls,
Death's quiet eddy off the roaring mart,
An oasis of peace, forgot, apart,
With muted strings the clamor on it falls;
And ghostly mists at dawn drop down like palls,
    Lithe bodies creep and slip into their heart,
    Half seen, half hid, across the mounds they dart.
Behold! On Beauty's grave a gaunt cat sprawls!
Beside some sage's stone their rage is fed—
    They stalk each other through the ragged grass;
    Snakelike they crawl where heroes long have lain;
With playful paw they pat the mouldering dead,
Grotesques that writhe and wail a devilish Mass—
    They're thoughts, life-clothed, sent forth by some dead brain!

[First published in *The Pleiades Club Year Book* (New York: Pleiades Club, 1911), 126.]

Illumination in the Mutant Rain Forest

Bruce Boston

Rebel saints and stray pariahs,
 clever con artists and stalwart desperadoes,
  mad adventurers and rogue fanatics,
devotees of all that is *outré* and fantastic . . .

embrace the transfigurations of this spacious borderland,
 this unexpected frontier where individual imaginations
  can chance freedom and death beyond
   the hermetic wisdom of dome-dweller cant,
beyond the futureless ghetto entrapment
of the unshielded urban sprawl . . .

where it is rumored that in a valley yet to be mapped,
somewhere in the vast interior of this organic labyrinth,
 light, the very *spiritus lux* incarnate,
  roams the treetop canopy silently
   from branch to intertwining branch . . .

spilling a liquid radiance from the cups of flowers,
 rifling the hidden plumage of exotic birds,
  peeling an ebon sheen
   from the chitinous backs of arboreal beetles . . .

gathering diverse shades and blending unseen colors
    to cast an illumination so archly pure
        in its dusk light clarity
    that it fills the leaves with a rarefied translucence
for miles in every direction . . .

so potent in its distillation
    you must smell and taste and savor
        its foxfire nectar with every intake of breath,
            so vital in the implications
        of its visionary promise
            that tears will rule your cheeks . . .

and you will know with a certainty akin to madness
    that all the unnamed appetites of your questing soul
        could soon be sated . . .

[First published in *Star*Line* (September 1989).]

Three Songs from *Nosferatu*

Dana Gioia

1. Ellen's Dream

I came to a table set for a feast,
Decked with silver and delicate lace.
The crystal shimmered in candlelight.
A long-stemmed rose adorned each place.
But the lace was torn and stained with rust,
The roses broken and bent askew.
The plates were empty. The room was cold,
And the only guest was you.

I heard the hush of a captured bird—
The twisted wings, the pounding heart.
A saw a fisherman take a knife
And carve his gleaming catch apart.
I watched the spider weave its web.
It sparkled in the beaded dew.
But when the moth lay in its trap,
I saw the prey was you.

I came down a stair to a bolted door.
I reached the lock, and it fell away.
I found a vast and sunless room.
I wanted to leave but had to stay.
The room was a chapel lit by candles,
But the cross had been broken in two.

The priest held a chalice of blood in his hands,
And on the altar was—you.

2. Nosferatu's Serenade

I am the image that darkens your glass,
The shadow that falls wherever you pass.
I am the dream you cannot forget,
The face you remember without having met.

I am the truth that must not be spoken,
The midnight vow that cannot be broken.
I am the bell that tolls out the hours.
I am the fire that warms and devours.

I am the hunger that you have denied,
The ache of desire piercing your side.
I am the sin you have never confessed,
The forbidden hand caressing your breast.

You've heard me inside you speak in your dreams,
Sigh in the ocean, whisper in screams.
I am the future you crave and you fear.
You know what I bring. Now I am here.

3. Mad Song

I sailed a ship
In the storm-wracked sea,
And all were drowned
Except for me.
I swam all night
Through death-cold waves
Till my shipmates called
From their sunken graves,
A lucky life for you, lad, a lucky life for you!

I fought through wars
In a barren land
Till none were left
Of my rugged band.
On a field of dead
Only I stood free.
Then a blind crow laughed
From a blasted tree,
A lucky life for you, lad, a lucky life for you!

I scaled a mountain
Of cold sharp stone.
The others fell,
And I climbed alone.
When I reached the top,

The winds were wild,
But a skull at my feet
Looked up and smiled,
A lucky life for you, lad, a lucky life for you!

[First published in Dana Gioia's *Nosferatu: An Opera Libretto*
(Minneapolis, MN: Graywolf Press, 2001), 32–34. Reprinted by
permission of the author.]

Articles

"Figures in a Nightmare"— The Poetry of Leah Bodine Drake: Part 2

Leigh Blackmore

II. Later Work

Between the ages of thirty-three and forty, Drake published four short stories: "Time and the Sphinx" (1947) in the *Magazine of Fantasy and Science Fiction*, "Foxy's Hollow" (1953) in *Fantasy Fiction*, and "Whisper Water" (May 1953) and "Mop-Head" (January 1954), both in *Weird Tales*. "Whisper Water" took the color cover illustration for the magazine, and also featured an impressive two-page internal black-and-white splash, all by artist Joseph Eberle. Dorothy McIlwraith was the editor of *Weird Tales* at the time.

Following publication of *A Hornbook for Witches*, Drake's poetry continued to appear in *Weird Tales* with "Revenant" (March 1951), "The Mermaid" (November 1952; illustrated), "Red Ghosts in Kentucky" (January 1953), "Six Merry Farmers" (September 1953), and "Out!" (March 1954 issue). *Weird Tales* was a dying market, and its last issue came out in September 1954. Drake then began to sell to Anthony Boucher at the *Magazine of Fantasy and Science Fiction* and published half a dozen or more poems there between 1954 and 1964, several of which were reprinted in Derleth's *Fire Sleet and Candlelight* (1961).

Around the same time Drake was selling to the *Magazine of Fantasy and Science Fiction*, her second volume of verse, *This Tilting Dust* (Francestown, NH: Golden Quill Press, 1955) was issued. At the time of publication, Drake was forty-one years old. The book gathered poems from numerous periodicals, among them the *Atlantic* (to which Drake was a frequent contributor), *Contemporary Poetry*, *Epos*, *Eve's Journal* (London), *Kaleidograph*, the *Lyric*, *Nature Magazine*, the *New Yorker*, *Poetry* (Chicago), *Poetry Chap-Book*, *Recurrence*, the *Saturday Review*, *Voices*, *Variegation*, and *Wings*. It contains 46 poems and, like many verse collections, is a slim volume of only 62 pages, issued in hardcover. (*Hornbook* ran to 70 pages.) The volume is dedicated to the poet's parents, Thomas Hulbert Drake and Cornelia Bodine Drake, and was a selection of the Book Club for Poetry. The jacket declares Drake to be "an acknowledged authority on witchcraft," and notes that her work has been greeted with delight by such seasoned poets as Marianne Moore, Edward Davison, Archibald Rutledge, and Margaret Widdemer among others. Edward Davison, the president of the Poetry Society of America, apparently was much impressed by Drake's abilities as a reader of her own verse: the back jacket flap tells us that he declared of one of her readings: "I haven't heard anyone read poetry like that since Dylan Thomas!" The jacket also commends her work as having the sensuous impact of Rilke and the extraordinary luminosity of Blake—high praise indeed. The volume won Drake the Borestone Mountain Poetry Award (she won the award once again later in her career) and the significant amount of $1,250. It was also a finalist in the National Book Foundation poetry awards for 1957.

This Tilting Dust is presented as a more "mainstream" volume of verse than *Hornbook*, which had been tailored to appeal to Arkham House's aficionados of horror and the fantastic. Many of the verses here are nature poetry, dealing with the changing seasons and with the natural world and its beauties, but the fantastic is far from absent.

The book's title derives from a line in the first poem, "Precarious Ground":

> And farmhouse windows burn
> Each with its tiny sun
> Against the tremendous night
> Arching this tilting dust
> That is a world in flight.

These lines almost recall a Clarkashtonian cosmic viewpoint! Drake ingeniously represents the microcosmic and the macrocosmic scale of things in a few lines and images. The small brave village is on precarious ground both because it stands "on a volcanic hill" and because of the "tilting dust" of Earth as it moves through its orbit. But here is also "the uncertain sand / Of the wild human heart."

Drake never loses sight of the human perspective, even when her verse deals with the mysteries of the universe or verges on the supernatural. The poet portrays love as building its "vulnerable towers" upon this sand, "the slope of old catastrophe." This poem won the Poetry Society's $300 first prize for the best poem in any magazine in the English-speaking world in 1955. It is certainly a memorable and impressive achievement.

Like *A Hornbook for Witches*, *This Tilting Dust* contains many poems centered on nature and the natural world. "Air" is an evocative poem about the element and its varied effects on us and the world. "Solar" is a brief triumphal hymn to the power of the Sun. "Luna" deftly explores the moon as influence on earth.

"The Final Green" is a lovely reflection on the colour green. Ultimately the work is a metaphor for mortality as witness its closing lines: "Earth's colour to which peoples pass / Under the final green of grass." "Rock and Bramble" is a simple allegory about the growth of our wisdom via difficult experience, and about the contrast between wisdom in youth and age.

"Fantasy in a Forest" is set by a pool in an Abyssinian wood, where animals including an elephant, a shy gazelle, a leopard, a camel, a serpent, and others mingle together, unafraid of one another as they drink from the pool. It is a utopian vision of peaceful coexistence. The unicorn "cleanses" and "blesses" the water. Water itself is usually a healing/cleansing image, but here the unicorn is a symbol for fantasy as a cleansing force.

"Drone" is a wonderful nature poem about the bee, rich in sensuous imagery:

> Gourmand of grapes, the wild vine wears his shadow,
> Rose and raspberry tangles cup him honey.
> He thinks the goldenrod's sweet waters only
> Distill for his delight and jewel the meadow!

"Cat Mummy" affectionately addresses the cat and laments the passing of the Egyptian age. In more nature-themed verse, Drake addresses various legends of the stork in "The Storks"; the dual nature of the spiteful snake in "Cobra"; and of the return of spring in "Wild

Geese in Spring." "Flemish Artists" relates how the Dutch artists painted biblical subjects but portrayed them with Flemish content, not depicting the real historical East.

"The Lazy Prince" is an amusingly quirky fairy tale, told with somewhat modern vernacular in which the prince *could* rescue a sleeping princess, but is too lazy:

> I'd attempt the rescue myself,
> Being her neighbour, if only that confounded briar
> Weren't so tough . . . and my armour's somewhere on a shelf . . .
> And I've heard the stairs are steep that lead to her bower.

"Childhood Summers" is a Bradburyesque nostalgic reflection on seasons past and the special fantasies of childhood. Likewise, "What Are the Little Girls Made Of?" is a superb poem memorializing the special, magical imaginings of childhood:

> We lived with imminent marvel! In some little room
> Of the sumac, secret, hushed with sun, the more-than-real
> Might appear: a talking beast out of Grimm
> Or the toad with the green gem blazing in his skull. . . .
>
> It is never wholly lost, that hope, nor quite outgrown:
> Old children, we half expect to see
> In one form or another the crowned swan
> Alight on the lake, the keyhole shine in a tree.

"The Undine" is perhaps one of Drake's strongest fantastic poems. In it she eloquently evokes "drowned forgotten temples," "red octopi and coral towns of death," and "pirates' bones that bloom with white and purple / anemones' soft feral funeral wreath." The undine finally rises, "green-haired, web-fingered, on the wave's long swell." In other verses, Drake conjures gods and goddesses of ancient times, as in "Semele," in which the goddess is made pregnant by the sky god, or "The Foam-Born," a paean to the goddess in her multifarious forms throughout the ages.

"Minor Poet" is a self-deprecating poem that seems to indicate Drake did not think highly of her own poetic work. It is perhaps disingenuous, since the very lines in which the narrator claims to be minor are invested with stunning imagery:

> Somewhere within these thickets nests
> The phoenix on the incense-tree,
> But not one feather from his breast
> Has drifted flamelike down to me.

Similarly, in "The Beaches Beyond Oblivion" the poet expresses the wish that "something I may say, some verse or rhyme" might wash up on the shore of beaches where sea-wrack from all the periods of history lies.

"Song Against Smallness" recalls themes of some of Clark Ashton Smith's verse. It praises the expansive and the exotic and decries the modernist fashion for the plain and the mundane:

> Lost, lost is love for all the fine and fair,
> The unique and the rare,
> Peacocks and ivory!
> The world can only see beauty in apes.

"Leonardo Before His Canvas" depicts da Vinci as imbued with marvelous fantastical imagination, yet afraid to put brush to canvas:

> The light, the perilous fires fade,
> The emerald is unbroken still:
> The god in me yet hangs betrayed
> By the old Judas of my will.

"Vestal" is a sexually symbolic poem in which the virginal attitudes of the titular character are momentarily encroached upon by one of Drake's typically pagan figures, a satyr, who comes "curious, shy, from outer lands"—the vestal's sole encounter with a being of real life force.

"Fool's Paradise" describes a potential paradise undermined by "the bleak damnations of terrible sand and the bones of the wilderness." "Incoming Tide," written in three-line stanzas of free verse, reflects on the transitory nature of things as footprints on the sand are wiped out, as "the tide besoms the shore's histories." "Through-Train," in like manner, deals with opportunities lost, as the narrator glimpses for a brief second the face that she was born to love in the midst of a carnival in a small town, before the onrushing train bears her away.

"Love Song" employs Drake's favorite mythic creatures—the undine, the unicorn, the hamadryad—to build a love lyric more direct than found in her other verse: "Insouciance witched me from my solemn hollow / Up to your arms' gay city, to delight / In the miraculous towers of your flesh." "Old Man on the Seashore" is a touching exploration of the treasures that an old man sees in the junk he gathers at the seashore, "that his life's fires may burn for one more day." The poet asks: "Are you searching for treasure from jeweled under-caves / That the ocean promised once, old man?— / A mermaid's looking glass, a living star, a lost crown?"

In "I Met a Lion," the narrator meets the noble beast, which is "good and mild / An innocent, huge and golden child." But she sends it back to the wilderness whence it came, for she cannot be friends with it: "Such peace would end / That darling fiction I embrace: / The overlordship of my race."

"We Come out of the Forest, Fearing Stars," in free verse, is about tribesmen whose forest canopies have been blown away by a tempest-year. They must emerge from the protective forest to face the threat of lions and the loss of their totems. "The Darkened Glass" is an effective meditation on the many ways in which human physical vision is limited, and yet imagination enables us to see "a world without end that glimpsed or guessed / Shines with no light of land or sea." "We Move on Turning Stone" closes out the collection with what seems an echo of "Precarious Ground"—a brief pondering of our smallness in the universe and our need to find light.

This Tilting Dust is not nearly as well-known a volume as A Hornbook for Witches, but contains numerous finely wrought poems of the macabre and fantastic, and is overall of a very high quality. Anyone who appreciates Drake's poetry or imaginative verse in general should certainly track down a copy.

Conclusion

The value of Leah Bodine Drake's poetry is indisputable. While the lack of wide variation in her meters may be considered a deficiency, her many merits—a fine way with imagery, her skillful word-choice, the richness and seemingly effortless potency of her compressed and vivid work—make her one of the most remarkable of weird poets of the twentieth century, and one whose work is too little-known. Indeed, the thematic compass of her admittedly small oeuvre, ranging as it does from weird to regional, from historical to fantastic, is testament to her status as a true poet, unrestricted by any single narrow genre and capable of encompassing themes of varied human interest.

The reputation of Leah Bodine Drake—newspaperwoman; drama, movie, and music critic; animal-lover; book collector; fictioneer and poet—is overdue for a revival. Her poetic work is certainly worthy of continued preservation and deserves rescue from comparative oblivion, to take its place at the forefront of macabre poetry. An enterprising publisher with a poetry line such as Hippocampus Press, Dark Regions Press, or PS Publishing should certainly seek to issue a collected volume of her work.

Reviews

Studies of Death

Michael Dirda

PARK BARNITZ. *The Book of Jade*. Compiled by David E. Schultz and Michael J. Abolafia. New York: Hippocampus Press, 2015. 328 pp. $20.00 tpb.

When a third, and significantly revised, edition of Karl Beckson's *Aesthetes and Decadents of the 1890s* was recently given to the world, I looked yet again on the contents page for Park Barnitz. His name was not there. True, his classic work *The Book of Jade* was published (anonymously) in 1901, and Beckson's anthology focuses almost entirely on British poets and prose writers. Nonetheless, some transplanted Americans are featured—Vincent O'Sullivan, most prominently—and it seems needlessly rigorous, not to say narrow-minded, to exclude Barnitz simply because he spent most of his short life (1878–1901) in Des Moines, Iowa.

The American poet's absence is all the more regrettable because he so obviously belongs in the same company as, say, Enoch Soames, the much written-about author of *Fungoids* and *Negations*. In fact, Barnitz's collected poems could well borrow Count Stenbock's blunt title, *Studies of Death*. In his later poetry, particularly, Barnitz regularly supplemented the sickly-sweet soliloquizings of a weary dissolute with ecstatic celebrations of wormy dissolution. Baudelaire—to whom *The Book of Jade* is dedicated—himself never approaches the necrophiliac exuberance of Barnitz in full spate. In paeans to putrefaction, the poet achieves—perhaps aims for—a ghoulish comedy. Surely Barnitz, the arch-connoisseur of "worm-ragout" and "cholera corpses weirdly black," rather than the eighteenth-century Robert Blair, more aptly deserves to be dubbed the head of the Graveyard School of poetry.

While early Romantic poets might find inspiration in crumbling ruins or beauty in the Medusa, Park Barnitz discovered his own inspiration first in spiritual ennui and then in physical decay. But, as I have hinted, to take his more gruesome outpourings seriously would be ludicrous. They are the Grand Guignol effusions of a young man aiming to shock. *Épater le bourgeois!* Or perhaps, *épater le père!* These poems are, in effect, wordier versions of "Greasy grimy gopher guts, / Mutilated monkey meat, / Tiny baby bird's feet / And me without a spoon!" Much of the *Book of Jade* cries out for illustration in the charnel baroque style of E.C. Comics' *Tales from the Crypt*:

> 2nd corpse: ". . . O foolish ragged-bones
> Woulds't thou show forth thy dripping excrements
> And shredded rottenness to the face of day?
> Stink and be still, and leave us here in peace.
> 1st corpse: "Envy me not, O stench, slop-face, dung-eyes;
> My bones are clean and dry as the tomb's walls,
> And stink not; as for thee, thou art a sink."

Happily, putrefaction is only one aspect of Barnitz's pessimism, misanthropy and poetry.

I myself vividly remember how I first heard the name Park Barnitz. In a video titled "An Interview with a Book Collector," Mark Valentine, the distinguished author, editor, and bibliophile, conducted a partial tour of his library. He spoke of favorite writers, several from the 1890s— Arthur Machen, Hubert Crackanthorpe—and his own ongoing quest for slim volumes of decadent verse. He then pulled out a copy of *The Book of Jade*, handling it with obvious affection and stressing that he'd never found another book of poetry quite like it. Valentine also remarked that he contributed an introduction to a facsimile of the original edition published by Durtro Press. Alas, even that issue is almost as expensive as the original 1901 printing, brought out in an edition of 600 copies by William Doxey "At the Sign of the Lark." One wonders if Barnitz smiled at this juxtaposition of the bird that sings at heaven's gate with his poetry's recurrent obsession with worms that gnaw a corpse's flesh.

I subsequently learned that *The Book of Jade* was available as an online text and duly bookmarked the site. But reading a poem—especially poems of this kind—on a screen seems, to use an odd word in this context, sacrilegious. The new Hippocampus paperback of *The Book of Jade* is, however, the next best thing to the first edition. Indeed, in several ways it may be preferable, since editors David E. Schultz and Michael J. Abolafia have enhanced the original's contents with uncollected poems and essays, as well as a short biography of Barnitz by Gavin Callaghan, and a dozen critical pieces about his work. The Hippocampus cover even replicates the striking art deco painting of the original boards. But who or what is that mysterious figure, carrying a sword and wrapped in swirling bands of cloth? Are they funeral cerements? Given the slightly jarring color combination—black, red, and greenish yellow—the whole suggests something forbidden, unhealthy, and probably as insidious as Robert W. Chambers's accursed *The King in Yellow.*

The Book of Jade is divided into two halves. In the first we are presented with world-weary reflections on life, sometimes in the persona of an Eastern potentate worn out by pleasure and dissipation:

> I am a little tired of all things mortal;
> I see through half-shut eyelids languorous
> The old monotonous
> Gold sun set slowly through the western portal,
> Where I recline upon my deep diwan
> In Ispahan.
>
> I am a little weary of the Persian
> Girl that I lov'd; I am quite tir'd of love;
> And I am weary of
> The smoking censers, and the sweet diversion
> Of stroking Leila's jasmine-scented hair,
> I thought so fair. . . .

Soon our etiolated narrator confesses that "nothing is very sad; nor wonderful, / nor beautiful." He ends his confession with one of several echoes of Mallarmé's famous line, "Je suis triste, hélas, et j'ai lu tous les livres" (I am sad, alas, and I have read all the books):

> Alas, all art, and knowledge, and all passion
> I have had; I have heard all the symphonies;

I have sailed all the seas;
I have drained all life's cup in languid fashion;
And I am come to Persia again,
Land of cocagne.

The poems in the first half of *The Book of Jade* keep up this fin-de-siècle listlessness, as their very titles make clear: "Opium," "Languor," "Ennui," "Hélas," "Autumn Song," "Poppy Song," "Liebes-Tod," "Nocturne." For the most part, though, Barnitz never produces memorable single lines, as do the best poets of the era. Certainly, none that approach, say, Dowson's "I have been faithful to thee, Cynara, in my fashion." But he often achieves a kind of sing-song mellifluousness: "I gaze through *sâd*-shaped eyelids languorous / Far off from Ispahan where roses blow." Sometimes, he can even manage—surprise!—the bounce of light verse:

To the girls of Persia, India, China, we know how to sigh;
If the heartless heart of Lili tedious cruel prove,
Go and dance the tarantella with the girls of Hokusai!"

Throughout Barnitz's collection, one senses a young poet trying out various forms, as in "Ballad," in which he echoes "Sir Patrick Spens": "And red her lips as the red red wine." Might he, for another example, be faintly remembering Horaces's "O matre pulchra filia pulchrior" (O fair mother of a fairer daughter) in such phrases as "she was more fair than all the lilies / Among the lilies, in the lily garden"? This is lovely, but other experiments, such as "Litany"—in which all the rhyme words are either "me" or "thee"—are ultimately tedious.

Still, Barnitz suffuses the first half of *The Book of Jade* with considerable Verlainean lyricism, as in these lines from its final poem, which also carries faint echoes of Baudelaire, particularly his prose poem "N'Importe ou Hors du Monde" (Anywhere out of the world):

"Come thou with me, beloved,
Come thou with heart unquailing
There where no ships come sailing,
Out of the dreary world.

Come thou with me, beloved,
Out of the world and its seeming,
Where all things are only dreaming,
And shadows all we know.

The second half of Barnitz's collection opens with the exquisite eeriness of "Mad Sonnet": "I am weary of seeing shapeless things that fly." Who wouldn't be? Better yet, one detects a proleptic Lovecraftian element when he then refers to "that lidless Eye / That comes and stares at me, O God of light!"

But, as this second half proceeds, the poems gradually move from the weird to the grotesque, from the decadent to the disgusting. Barnitz reworks Richard Lovelace's famous line "I could not love you, dear, so much, loved I not honor more" into the brutal shock of "I could not love you more if you were dead." He sounds an even more coffin-like hammering in "The Grave": "Dead, dead, dead, dead, dead, dead, dead, dead, dead, dead." Yet just when one tires of hearing that blunt word over and over, Barnitz almost makes it sound lyrical through alliteration and assonance in "The Grotesques": "Within those dead dominions the dead tsar / Receiv'd his plaudits where dead bodies are."

Despite the valiant efforts of Gavin Callaghan to fill out the poet's biography, there's just not a lot known about Park Barnitz. His father was a prominent Lutheran evangelist who spent much of his time on the road. One year he was home for only three weeks. Samuel Bacon Barnitz was, in short, a believer, not a blasphemer. Might his son's poems have been a way of cocking a snook at his father's religiosity? Maybe. Park did live at home but, from all accounts, he seemed to be comfortable there and devoted to his sisters and mother. One can hardly imagine how the family would have reacted to *The Book of Jade*. More likely than not, its poems were largely composed while Barnitz was a student of Asian studies at Harvard, where he earned a B.A. and M.A. That said, the young versifier seems to have made little impression on his fellow students, one of whom would later rank among the greatest figures in American poetry, Wallace Stevens.

What authors did Barnitz read? From the evidence of the essay "The Art of the Future," he was aware of contemporary art and literature from around the world. His prose can be, at times, nearly aphoristic: "The important thing is not to belong to a school, but to produce a masterpiece." (He sounds quite like Cyril Connolly in his analysis of modern writing, *Enemies of Promise*.) In his article Barnitz speaks highly of Paul Verlaine, as well he might. But he also viewed George Meredith as "the most truly creative mind in English letters after Shakespeare," which wouldn't seem quite so absurd had he said Dickens instead. Like Max Beerbohm, whose early work he also knew, Barnitz greatly disliked Kipling—see the essay "The Truth about Rudyard Kipling"—largely because of his jingoism. Neither of these aesthetes seem to have recognized Kipling's amazing inventiveness and energy, his storytelling power and flair for memorable lines of poetry. Sadly, Kipling's masterpiece, the incomparable *Kim*, came out just after Barnitz's essay ran in the *Goose-Quill*. Almost needless to say, this younger epicure of the terrible pays homage to Poe, but it is a surprise to see him sing the praises of the rumbustious, healthy-minded Walt Whitman.

There's so much we would like to know about Barnitz. Did he read, for instance, Beckford's *Vathek*? This novel would seem one of the precursors of *The Book of Jade*, interlacing Oriental languor, excess, and horror. Various early reviewers suggest the influence Omar Khayyam. Perhaps. Did Barnitz take drugs, as some have thought? Did he die of a heart attack, as his obituary suggested, or might this merely be a convenient fiction to disguise suicide?

Upon first reading *The Book of Jade* I found it a grave, so to speak, disappointment. Indeed, one reason I started this piece with a pastiche of the opening to Max Beerbohm's "Enoch Soames" is that I thought Barnitz rather laughable or at least sophomoric in his impulse for the gross-out. But when I reread the poems I had liked best, I found their sickly sweet fin-de-siècle lyricism increasingly attractive. The essays at the back of the Hippocampus critical edition also made me look more again at Barnitz's work. One piece, by the horror writer Joseph Payne Brennan, is astutely evenhanded: "Of the 59 poems in the book, about a dozen are worth salvaging. When contrasted with the best, the worst are really bad." I'd have to agree.

In the end, Park Barnitz showed more promise than achievement and he can hardly be ranked with Dowson or Verlaine, let alone his book's dedicatee Charles Baudelaire. But then he was only twenty-three when he died: His youthful posturings, the trying out of different poetic forms, and even his boneyard banter make up some of what one might call, oddly enough, his charm. So, after some hesitation, I will shelve my copy of *The Book of Jade* with the slim volumes written by other members of what Yeats once called "the tragic generation." You might want to do the same.

Two from Eldritch

D. L. Myers

PETER ADAM SALOMON. *Prophets*. San Antonio, TX: Eldritch Press, 2014. 107 pp. $5.38 tpb.
ROSE BLACKTHORN. *Thorns, Hearts and Thistles*. San Antonio, TX: Eldritch Press, 2015. 100 pp. $5.99 tpb.

I hadn't read anything by Peter Adam Salomon before receiving his book for review, and after reading the forty-six poems that make up *Prophets* I'm not encouraged to read more. I found the poems to be very subjective, lacking clear images, and difficult to understand. They are largely unpunctuated, and what punctuation there is didn't assist me in clarifying their meaning. His use of layout also did not improve my understanding. The poems are primarily written in unmetered prose, and the few poems that did use rhyme schemes I found awkward and ineffective.

Madness, murder, and suicide seemed to be the primary topics of the poems, but I didn't find anything compelling or interesting in his portrayals. They seemed to be the vague, delusional ramblings of the mentally ill instead of poetry. As in this excerpt from "Alliterations . . . into Insanity":

> across a crowded room
> I see you—
> I start to smile . . .
>
> into the intricacies of insanity
> dip the soul into celluloid
> tears run down the face of statues in the park

> beauty crawls beneath creativity
> weaving wicked tapestries within sanity
> lying to the liar in my mind . . .

I would take a pass on *Prophets*. There is too much good dark poetry being written today to spend time reading it.

In contrast, I was impressed by the imagery of "Enamored in Darkness," the first poem in Rose Blackthorn's collection, and how that imagery is used to create an atmosphere of apprehension and dread.

> Once I placed a mirror
> casually, lazily leaned against the closet
> and a dim kiddie nightlight
> puddled amber syrup on the floor
> that night there was no sleeping
> as I waited for the rustle
> of withered and twisted appendage
> among the dust-bunnies and dead spiders

The poem also raised my expectations for the rest of the book. Unfortunately, the remainder of the poems did not fully live up to those expectations. Every poem contained at least one notable image, as in this example from "A Drive at Dusk":

> little girls giggling as butterflies wobble
> in the pollen dusted air of afternoon

but they were uneven in their effectiveness and only a few rose to the level of the first.

The majority of the poems are in unmetered prose, but in a few Blackthorn uses rhyme schemes that are fairly successful, although the meter is off, making some of the lines a bit clumsy. Her subject matter ranges from tales of ghostly visitations to failed relationships, lost souls, and an interesting take on the succubus.

This is her first collection, and by and large I think it is mostly successful. It definitely has enticed me to look for more of her poetry in the future.

Notes on Contributors

Carole Abourjeili started writing poetry in Arabic and French in Lebanon; then, a few years after migrating to Australia at age twelve, she began writing in English. Most of her poems deal with the supernatural and what lies beyond the known: "Each poem is a piece of my soul that I like to share with the world. For me, writing is a place where I find inner peace and connection with the Divine."

Linda D. Addison is the award-winning author of four collections of poetry and prose and the first African-American recipient of the Bram Stoker Award. She has published more than 300 poems, stories, and articles and is a member of CITH, HWA, SFWA and SFPA.

Mike Allen's debut collection of short stories, *Unseaming*, was a finalist for the 2014 Shirley Jackson Award. Other recent books include a poetry collection, *Hungry Constellations*. Arts columnist for the daily newspaper in Roanoke, Virginia, by day, he is also the editor and publisher of Mythic Delirium Books. In May 2015 he raised $12,000 through Kickstarter to produce *Clockwork Phoenix 5*.

David Barker has been a fan of weird literature all his life. Recently, his writings have appeared in *Fungi*, *Cyäegha*, and *Shoggoth.net*. In collaboration with W. H. Pugmire, David has had two books published by Dark Renaissance Books: *The Revenant of Rebecca Pascal* (2014) and *In the Gulfs of Dream and Other Lovecraftian Tales* (2015).

Leigh Blackmore has written weird verse since age thirteen. He has lived in the Illawarra, New South Wales, Australia, for the last decade. He has edited *Terror Australis: Best Australian Horror* (1993) and *Midnight Echo 5* (2011) and written *Spores from Sharnoth & Other Madnesses* (2008). A nominee for SFPA's Rhysling Award (Best Long Poem), Leigh is also a four-time Ditmar Award nominee. He is currently compiling his second collection of fantastic verse and writing a thriller novel.

Adam Bolivar, a native of Boston, now residing in Portland, Oregon, has had his weird fiction and poetry appear in the pages of *Nameless*, the *Lovecraft eZine*, *Spectral Realms*, and Chaosium's *Steampunk Cthulhu* and *Atomic Age Cthulhu* anthologies. His first book, *The Fall of the House of Drake*, was published by Dunhams Manor Press in 2015.

Bruce Boston is the author of fifty books and chapbooks, including the novels *The Guardener's Tale* and *Stained Glass Rain*. His poetry has received the Bram Stoker Award, the *Asimov's* Readers Award, and the Rhysling and Grandmaster Awards of the SFPA. His fiction has received a Pushcart Prize and twice been a finalist for the Bram Stoker Award (novel, short story). His latest collection, *Resonance Dark and Light*, is available from Eldritch Press.

Jason V Brock has been widely published in anthologies, online, comics, and magazines (*Weird Fiction Review*, S. T. Joshi's *Black Wings* series, *Fangoria*, and many others). An award-winning filmmaker and publisher, he is also editor-in-chief of a website/print digest called [NameL3ss]. Along with his wife, Sunni, he is a herp, tech consultant, and health nut.

Pat Calhoun works from an old house in Santa Rosa, California, that he shares with his wife, three cats, and a large collection of fantasy books. He wrote a column, "Weird Words," about vintage fantasy comics, that ran for fifteen years in *Comic Book Marketplace* and currently writes for the *International Netsuke Society Journal*. He is also busy editing *Weird and Wondrous: An Anthology of Fantasy Poems*, and writing a few of them as well.

G. O. Clark's writing has been published in *Asimov's Science Fiction*, *Analog*, *Space & Time*, *A Sea of Alone: Poems for Alfred Hitchcock*, *Tales of the Talisman*, *Daily SF*, and more. He is the author of eleven poetry collections, most recently *Gravediggers' Dance* (2014). His fiction collection *The Saucer Under My Bed and Other Stories* was published in

2011. He was a Bram Stoker Award finalist in poetry in 2011. He lives in Davis, California.

Dan Clore is the author of *The Unspeakable and Others* (H. Harksen Productions, 2009), a collection of avant-garde Gothic stories; *Weird Words: A Lovecraftian Lexicon* (Hippocampus Press, 2009), a dictionary of the genre with extensive illustrative quotations; and critical essays on H. P. Lovecraft, Clark Ashton Smith, and others.

C. S. E. Cooney is a Rhode Island writer, actor, poet, and singer-songwriter. She is the author of the Dark Breakers series: *The Breaker Queen* and *The Two Paupers*. "Witch, Beast, Saint," the first erotic fairy tale in her Witch's Garden series, can be found at *Strange Horizons*, while her second, *The Witch in the Almond Tree*, is available for purchase on Amazon. Cooney's first short fiction collection, *Bone Swans*, is forthcoming from Mythic Delirium Books in July 2015.

Margi Curtis (MCA) is a witch, writer, artist, healer and activist, living in Wollongong, New South Wales, Australia. Published in magazines and anthologies, in print and online, she is the author of four collections of poetry. Her poem "A Deathless Love" appeared in *Midnight Echo* No 5 (AHWA, 2011).

Shirley Jackson Award finalist **Nicole Cushing** is the author of the novel *Mr. Suicide*, the short story collection *The Mirrors*, and multiple stand-alone novellas. Her work has garnered praise from such diverse sources as Thomas Ligotti, *Famous Monsters of Filmland*, John Skipp, S. T. Joshi, Jack Ketchum, Poppy Z. Brite, Ray Garton, and *Ain't It Cool News*. A native of Maryland, she now lives with her husband in Indiana.

Ashley Dioses is a writer of dark fiction and poetry from Southern California. She is currently working on her first book of weird poetry. Her poetry has appeared in *Weird Fiction Review* #5 (Centipede Press,

2014) and *Spectral Realms* Nos. 1 and 2 (Hippocampus Press, 2014–15), and a few will appear in K. A. Opperman's *The Crimson Tome* (Hippocampus Press, 2015), *Xnoybis* #2 (Dunhams Manor Press, 2015), and elsewhere.

Michael Dirda is a weekly book columnist for *The Washington Post*. He is the author, most recently, of the 2012 Edgar Award-winning *On Conan Doyle* and the 2015 collection of essays, *Browsings: A Year of Reading, Collecting, and Living with Books*.

Ian Futter began writing stories and poems in his childhood, but only lately has started to share them. One of his poems appears in Jason V Brock's anthology *The Darke Phantastique* (Cycatrix Press, 2014), and he continues to produce dark fiction for admirers of the surreal.

Liam Garriock is an upcoming writer, poet, and prose-poet in the tradition of Poe, Machen, Blackwood, and Lovecraft. He is a passionate enthusiast of the fantastic, esoteric, and grotesque. This poem marks his first published weird work. Garriock lives in Edinburgh, whence he dreams of mystical phantasies, horrors, and visions.

Stanley Gemmell is a Puerto Rican poet and musician living in Providence, RI. He regularly posts his poetry online and runs several writing blogs. His poetry has appeared in *The Rush-Ins Poetry Reader* (Koja Press, 2000), *The Alembic Literary Journal*, *Urban Spaghetti* and elsewhere.

Wade German's poems have appeared in journals and anthologies such as *Cyäegha*, *Hypnos*, *Space and Time*, *Weird Fiction Review*, *Zymbol*, *A Darke Phantastique* (Cycatrix Press), *Avatars of Wizardry* (P'rea Press), and previous issues of *Spectral Realms*. His poetry collection *Dreams from a Dark Nebula*, nominated for the Elgin Award, is available from Hippocampus Press.

Dana Gioia has published four volumes of poetry, most recently *Pity the Beautiful* (2012), three volumes of criticism, and two opera libretti; he has also edited several volumes of poetry. He served as chairman of the National Endowment for the Arts from 2002 to 2009. In 2014 he won the Aiken Taylor Award for Modern American Poetry.

Bram Stoker Award–nominated author **Chad Hensley** had his first book of poetry, *Embrace the Hideous Immaculate* (Raw Dog Screaming Press), published in May 2014. His recent poetry appearances include *Space and Time* #122, *Weird Fiction Review* #5, the *Pedestal Magazine* #74, and *Spectral Realms* #1 and #2. His short story "A Clicking in the Shadows," cowritten with W. H. Pugmire, appears in *Inhuman* #6.

A prolific writer, editor, and small-press publisher since the 1970s, **Randall D. Larson** has also written short stories, most with Lovecraftian angles, which appeared in a number of small-press terror tale volumes. Larson has recently begun exploring the format of haiku, corrupted into what he calls Cthaiku, in delineating the weird sense of horror in this poetic pattern. Recent weird tales have appeared in Allen Koszowski's *Inhuman*, the *Lovecraft eZine*, and elsewhere.

Charles Lovecraft created P'rea Press (www.preapress.com) to publish weird, fantastic, and supernatural poetry and nonfiction. An admirer of formalist verse, he seeks to foster and keep alive that rich ongoing tradition. His work has appeared in *Nyctalops*, *Fantasy Tales*, and *Weird Fiction Review*, and a sonnet cycle is forthcoming in *Black Wings IV* (PS Publishing, 2015).

Reiss McGuinness is a photographer and poet living in Bath. His poetry often deals with the politics and nature of the world, his haiku with hesitation, nostalgia, and mistakes. His haiku recently was featured in the Fringe Arts Bath festival. As Rabban, his photography practice involves dark and surreal images that portray estrangement and otherness.

Mark McLaughlin's writings have appeared in hundreds of magazines, websites, and anthologies, including *Galaxy, Living Dead 2, Cemetery Dance, Midnight Premiere, Dark Arts,* and two volumes of *The Year's Best Horror Stories* (DAW). Collections of his fiction include *Best Little Witch-House in Arkham, Beach Blanket Zombie,* and *Hideous Faces, Beautiful Skulls.* With co-authors Rain Graves and David Niall Wilson, he won the Bram Stoker Award for poetry for *The Gossamer Eye.*

John Mundy was born in a coal mining/railroading Pennsylvania town; discovered "The Raven" at five, Lovecraft and Beaumont at eight, and his fate was sealed. Three years ago, he was forced into physical inactivity from a leg injury that left him bored and depressed; and much to his surprise, he began to write poems and short stories. Thanks to his young and talented friend, Liam, he discovered *Spectral Realms* and decided to submit a few pieces. Everything after was a pleasant surprise!

D. L. Myers's poetry has appeared in *Spectral Realms* #1 and #2. His influences include H. P. Lovecraft, Clark Ashton Smith, Robert E. Howard, George Sterling, Algernon Blackwood, and Arthur Machen. He dwells among the mist-shrouded hills and farms of the Skagit Valley in the Pacific Northwest with his partner and a pack of demon badger hounds.

K. A. Opperman is a poet with a predilection for the strange, the Gothic, and the grotesque, continuing the macabre and fantastical tradition of such luminaries as Poe, Clark Ashton Smith, and H. P. Lovecraft. His first verse collection, *The Crimson Tome,* was published by Hippocampus Press in 2015.

Fred Phillips's first collection of poetry, *From the Cauldron,* was published by Hippocampus Press in 2010; a second collection, *Winds from Sheol,* is under way. He has been published in the *Cimmerian, Studies in the Fantastic, Weird Fiction Review,* and elsewhere.

Ann K. Schwader lives and writes in Colorado. Her most recent book is *Dark Energies* (P'rea Press, 2015). Her *Wild Hunt of the Stars* (Sam's Dot, 2010) was a Bram Stoker Award finalist. She is also a 2010 Rhysling Award winner and the Poet Laureate for NecronomiCon Providence 2015.

Darrell Schweitzer is a short story writer and novelist, and former co-editor of *Weird Tales*. He has published much humorous Lovecraftian verse (*Non Compost Mentis* [Zadok Allen, 1993] et al.) and also has two serious poetry collections in print, *Groping Toward the Light* (Wildside Press, 2000) and *Ghosts of Past and Future* (Wildside Press, 2008).

Marge Simon's works appear in publications such as *DailySF Magazine*, *Pedestal*, and *Urban Fantasist*. She edits a column for the HWA Newsletter, "Blood & Spades: Poets of the Dark Side," and serves as Chair of the Board of Trustees. She won the Strange Horizons Readers Choice Award, 2010, and the SFPA's Dwarf Stars Award, 2012. She has won three Bram Stoker Awards for Superior Work in Poetry and has poetry in the HWA anthology *It's Scary Out There* (Simon & Schuster, 2015).

Oliver Smith's writing has appeared in anthologies published by the Inkerman Press, Ex Occidente Press, and Dark Hall Press.

Christina Sng is a poet, writer, and occasional toymaker. Her poems have appeared many venues, such as *Mythic Delirium*, *Space and Time*, and *Tales of the Talisman*, and have received several honorable mentions in *The Year's Best Fantasy and Horror* as well as two Rhysling nominations. In her free time, she plays the ukulele, dreams of exploring the Andromeda nebula, and carves out poems in longhand, imbibing an aromatic cup of tea.

Jason Sturner grew up in northeastern Illinois and now lives near the Great Smoky Mountains in Tennessee. Sturner has been a naturalist, botanist, and, more recently, a stay-at-home dad. His stories and poems have appeared in *Space and Time*, *Star*Line*, *Tales of the Talisman*, and *Mythic Delirium*, among others. He has been nominated twice for a Rhysling Award, and a compilation of his best work is forthcoming.

Verse by Providence native **Jonathan Thomas** has consisted mostly of lyrics for country singer Angel Dean, Manhattan bands Escape by Ostrich and Fish & Roses, Swedish quartet scumCrown, and his own Septimania. His prose collections include *Midnight Call* (2008), *Tempting Providence* (2010), *Thirteen Conjurations* (2013), and *Dreams of Ys and Other Invisible Worlds* (2015), all from Hippocampus Press.

DJ Tyrer is the person behind Atlantean Publishing, which publishes the Yellow Leaves and Xothic Sathlattae poetry series and the Buxton University Press imprint. He has had work in such publications as *Sorcery & Sanctity: A Homage to Arthur Machen*, *Tales of the Dark Arts*, *Fossil Lake*, *Fossil Lake II*, and *Steampunk Cthulhu*, as well as having a Yellow Mythos novella available in paperback and on Kindle, *The Yellow House*.

Don Webb has been nominated for the Rhysling award and the International Horror Critics Award. He hopes to miss out winning other awards. His poetry chapbook, *Anubis on Guard* (Dark Regions Press, 1998), became valuable and collectible after he gave away his copies. He held a poetic license for years, but lost it for writing a sonnet in haiku-only zone.

M. F. Webb is pleased to reenter the world of writing and publication after a two-decade-long, journalism-induced hiatus. Originally from Texas, with degrees from Texas Christian University and the University of Texas at Arlington, she has made her home in Seattle for the past sixteen years.

Mary Krawczak Wilson has written poetry, fiction, plays, articles, and essays. She was born in St. Paul, Minnesota, and moved to Seattle in 1991. Her most recent essay appeared in the *American Rationalist*.

www.ingramcontent.com/pod-product-compliance
Lightning Source LLC
Chambersburg PA
CBHW051841090426
42736CB00011B/1921